Haunts of the Southwest

Haunts of the Southwest

Linda Moffitt

Schiffer Publishing Ltd
4880 Lower Valley Road, Atglen, Pennsylvania 19310

Dedication

For Hailey, my shining star.

Acknowledgments

I wish to thank everyone who helped me put this book together and the many more who took the time to tell me their spirited stories across the Southwest, as well as the NFL who gave me countless guilt-free Sunday's for writing.

Text by the author
Photos by R.W. O'Brien unless otherwise noted.
(Some photos by author, www.bigstockphotos.com, Library of Congress, J. O'Brien, and Josh Bond; All Random Photos Courtesy of R.W. O'Brien, except for Random 21 and 28 Courtesy of J. O'Brien)

Library of Congress Control Number: 2010929866

Designed by Mark David Bowyer
Type set in !Sketchy Times / New Baskerville BT

ISBN: 978-0-7643-3597-6
Printed in China

Schiffer Books are available at special discounts for bulk purchases for sales promotions or premiums. Special editions, including personalized covers, corporate imprints, and excerpts can be created in large quantities for special needs. For more information contact the publisher:

Published by Schiffer Publishing Ltd.
4880 Lower Valley Road
Atglen, PA 19310
Phone: (610) 593-1777; Fax: (610) 593-2002
E-mail: Info@schifferbooks.com

For the largest selection of fine reference books on this and related subjects, please visit our web site at www.schifferbooks.com
We are always looking for people to write books on new and related subjects.
If you have an idea for a book please contact us at the above address.

This book may be purchased from the publisher.
Include $5.00 for shipping.
Please try your bookstore first.
You may write for a free catalog.

In Europe, Schiffer books are distributed by
Bushwood Books
6 Marksbury Ave.
Kew Gardens
Surrey TW9 4JF England
Phone: 44 (0) 20 8392-8585; Fax: 44 (0) 20 8392-9876
E-mail: info@bushwoodbooks.co.uk
Website: www.bushwoodbooks.co.uk

Contents

Introduction 6

Arizona

Bisbee 8
Colossal Cave 14
Douglas 15
Flagstaff 17
Grand Canyon 19
Jerome 21
Nogales 29
Prescott 29
Superstition Mountains 30
Tombstone 34
Tucson 43
Vulture Mine 44
Yuma 45

California

Bodie 48
Calico 59
Death Valley 61
Tommy Knockers 66

Colorado

Durango 67
Mesa Verde 72
St. Elmo 75
Trinidad 77

Nevada

Carson City 78
Genoa 82
Gold Hill 85
Goldfield 89
Ruby Mountains 90
Virginia City 93

New Mexico

Albuquerque 102
Alcalde 105
Cimarron 106
Cloudcroft 109
Cuchillo 110
Elizabethtown 113
Granite Gap 116
Lincoln 118
Mesilla 122
Raton 123
Route 666 125
Santa Fe 127
Taos 133

Utah

Dead Horse State Park 138
Lake Powell 144
Minersville 145
Nephi 145
Silver Reef 148

Conclusion 150

Bibliography 151

Index 157

Introduction

According to the reference dictionary, southwest is the ordinal direction halfway between south and west. In the United States, the Southwestern states are New Mexico, Arizona, California, Nevada, Utah, and Colorado.

The Southwest conjures up images of cactus dotting the desert landscape, adobe pueblos, Indians weaving blankets, and chili peppers strung out to dry. I tried to keep to what I thought was the southwest; many of my stories are located in the desert areas of the region where the weather is hot, dry, and unforgiving.

My childhood memories are from vacations to the Southwest, driving countless hours to some remote spot and then waiting so my father could take a picture of something boring in just the right light. Along the way, I saw many things and went to places the average tourist may not have chosen to go. Old abandoned towns, stale antique stores, out of the way greasy spoons, dusty museums, and some of the most spectacular sites the country could offer. Somewhere between driving on the edge of a cliff in a motor home in Death Valley while the cassette player blasted the *Star Wars* soundtrack or being sprayed with the old fire truck's hose in Silverton, Colorado on the 4th of July. Eventually, I started to like these trips and wanted to see more and learn more about the history of these places we visited on vacation.

Over the years I have visited and collected many stories and experiences from the Southwest, lots of them I recount for you in this book; some were told to me by crusty old men who are long gone to their grave, and yet other stories are just a few years old. Several are legends, others talk of places that are located in areas that even the most experienced adventurer would not want to go, and some may be in your backyard. I have tried to put together a range of stories in places that make me think *Southwest*. Some of the haunting comes from towns in which almost every building has a ghost story attached, and then there is just the single haunted location. There are a few roads, bridges, and mountains that I talk about and even a river or two.

La Llorena is all over the Southwest; many of you have heard her story and some of you are telling that story to your children. No matter if you are just trying to keep them away from the dangerous river waters or you had an experience and are recounting that frightful night to your children, the wailing woman who lost her children still may be out there and looking for *your* children. In *Haunts of the Southwest* La Llorena is in New Mexico, a bitter old woman who rises out of rivers wailing for her children, mistaking innocent modern-day children for her own.

Stories of La Llorena are a small part of the tales that flourish around the Southwest. Tales are told about Billy the Kid haunting Lincoln County Courthouse, eerie occurrences in Bodie, California, where one empty house smells of lasagna. You will read about the clues to the Lost Dutchman's Mine and the dangers of the Superstition Mountains. And I must not forget to tell you about the giants of the Grand Canyon and what to look out for while driving on Route 666.

There are a few places you can visit or even stay in—hotels, restaurants, museums—there are other locations that are private; ghost enthusiasts and visitors are not welcome. I've included addresses of the public locations, but remember if you choose to visit some of the places I talk about, please be respectful of the living and the dead, obey all signs, do not trespass, and be careful. Ghosts do not usually hurt people; people get hurt by being frightened and falling down or tripping as they are running away.

While I enjoy the southwestern scenery to no end, it's the mystery of the southwest that draws me to it. Not too many locations in the world have so many unusual places. Let me just pose this question to you, where else can you see a ghost in the alien capital of the world?

Arizona

Bisbee

Known as the "Queen of the Copper Camps," Bisbee was founded in 1880. The Copper Queen Mine produced close to eight billion pounds of copper, but don't forget the gold, silver, lead, and zinc that was pulled from the Mule Mountains. The town was actually not that rough, but like all towns, the miners needed a place to blow off steam. Brewery Gulch was packed full of saloons with entertainment and the soiled doves who offered up their goods nightly; the area was the "liveliest spot between El Paso and San Francisco." The town you see today was mainly built in 1910 following a fire which destroyed the area around Main Street in 1908. Most of the mines closed in the 1970s but the town still thrives with artistic talent that has preserved the past.

Copper Queen Hotel

The Copper Queen Hotel opened in 1902. The Phelps Dodge Mining Company built the hotel for investors and businessmen involved with the mine to come and relax in luxury. Offering seventy-three rooms with a shared bath at the end of each hallway, the hotel has been updated since and each of the forty-eight rooms now offers their own private bath. The five-story hotel was originally built as four stories but in 1944, the hotel purchased an elevator and added the fifth floor to house the mechanics of the elevator.

Spirits have been seen looking out of the windows at the Copper Queen Hotel. *Courtesy of R.W. O'Brien*

The hotel offers up an array of ghosts—from the prostitute that frightens male guests who stay in her room to a little boy who plays pranks on unsuspecting guests. The activity is so great, the hotel offers a ghost register, and every Thursday night, there's a ghost hunt of the hotel.

The Copper Queen Hotel states there are three ghosts currently residing at the hotel. The most famous one is Julia Lowell and a room is named after her. She was a former prostitute in Bisbee and sometimes entertained customers at the hotel. According to the hotel, she foolishly fell in love with one of her customers and when he found out, he wanted nothing more to do with her. Julia was so heartbroken she committed suicide in one of the rooms at the hotel.

Julia is known to whisper in men's ears and some have even seen her appear before them as a white misty form. If you are a man staying alone in her room, she is known to tickle guests' feet or performs a naked dance at the foot of the bed.

Another ghost residing at the hotel is that of an older gentleman. He is reported to be quite dapper dressed in a cape and top hat with long hair and a well-groomed beard. He has been seen hanging out in doorways or in the corner of a room; a smell of cigar smoke follows this gentleman around in the hotel.

The ghost of a young boy plays pranks in the lobby of the Copper Queen Hotel.
Courtesy of R.W. O'Brien

Spirits can be seen all over the Grand Canyon. *Courtesy of Library of Congress, HAER ARIZ, 3-GRACAN, 11-3*

Still another is the ghost of a young boy who is around eight or nine years old. His mother or father was employed in the hotel at the time of his drowning in the San Pedro River. Guests report their belongings being moved around in their rooms, the feeling of being watched while in the shower, and hearing his little footsteps running down the hallways.

If you plan on visiting or staying at the Cooper Queen Hotel make sure to look for windows opening and closing on their own. Doors are known to lock by themselves and door handles sometimes open with no earthly hands to turn the knob. Sounds of a woman singing have been reported in and around the second floor rooms. Some employees have reported the elevator malfunctioning, the door jamming, and voices being heard inside when no one was aboard the elevator, and not to forget the transparent gentleman wearing old west garb that appears nightly by the piano in the bar.

Copper Queen Hotel
11 Lowell Avenue
Bisbee, AZ 85603
(520) 432-2216
www.copperqueen.com

Brewery Gulch

Brewery Gulch was the pit of Bisbee where men went to spend their hard-earned money and blow off steam. At that time, Bisbee did not have a sanitation system, all the human waste, rotting food, dead maggot-filled animals flowed down Brewery Gulches' streets and alleyways. Many miners and prostitutes still fill the streets of the Brewery Gulch district, but it's their ghosts who walk there. Tourists and locals report hearing footsteps following them as they make their way to their destination in the Gulch.

Another more gruesome ghost that is reported being seen is that of a woman whose eye sockets are crawling with worms, keeping company with the woman whose head is adorned with an axe that inevitably must have killed her. There is also a man who sits in a chair outside a house with what appears to be a large hole in his torso. Many other sightings have been reported as well that are more mundane, the cleaning woman who has been seen mailing a letter at the post office only to vanish soon after, or the Indian chief that walks the streets before dawn.

Oliver House

The Oliver House was built in 1909 by the wife of mining tycoon Henry Oliver. Edith Oliver designed the house as a boarding house and offices for the Calumet and Arizona Mining Company. The house started out innocent enough, but through the years, it has had a violent and bloody history.

February 22, 1920, Nathan Anderson was shot in the head and back at the top of the staircase as he was entering room number thirteen. His murderer was never captured and to this day remains an unsolved mystery. Another version of this same story states that Nathan was having an affair with the wife of a local policeman. On that fateful day, Nathan was shot between the eyes upon entering room thirteen. Then the vengeful husband aimed his gun at his wife killing her. He headed downstairs killing the rest of the occupants of the house who had congregated in the parlor. Upon this shooting spree, he drove to the edge of town and shot himself.

I think the first version of the story is a more accurate account of what happened. In either version, the house has had a total of twenty-seven people die within its walls, natural or unnatural.

An elderly presence sits in the front window of the Oliver House watching guests arrive. *Courtesy of R.W. O'Brien*

The spirit of an elderly lady seems to keep watch in the Oliver House. Her spirit has been seen sitting in her rocking chair in the front window watching time pass. If the chair is moved away from the window she will gently move it back into place. A total of five spirits have been identified as residing in the Oliver House.

The house was sold in 1986 to a skeptic. He soon found out spirits exist, at least in his house. His first night alone in the house resulted in hearing footsteps that continued from the hallway through the locked door and right up to his bed. The new owner heard water running through pipes that were no longer there and doors that opened and closed by themselves.

Oliver House
24 Sowles Avenue
Bisbee, AZ 85603
(520) 432-1900
www.bisbeeoliverhouse.com

Colossal Cave

Take a short fifteen mile drive out of Tucson and you will come upon Colossal Cave Mountain Park. The cave was discovered in 1879, when a local rancher was searching for stray cattle. He felt a cool breeze coming through a small hole and thought it may have been a lost mine; instead, it was a huge cavernous system that as of today still has not been fully explored. It was not long after that, a group of train robbers thought it would be a perfect hiding spot. In 1887, three outlaws relieved a train of three thousand dollars, taking cover in the cave system. A thirty-one-man posse guarded the entrance for two weeks, thinking the robbers would finally give themselves up. The posse waited patiently only to find out the outlaws had found another way out and had escaped.

Even though the outlaws found their way out, there are plenty of ghosts that either perished in the caves or just they like the ambiance. One such spirit is that of a young Indian maiden who, while trying to escape from a bear, crawled through a small hole in the rocks only to find herself on a ledge twelve feet above the ground below. She was never seen again. Did she die in the fall, or injuries received from the fall? Maybe once she got into the cave, she could not find her way out and starved to death. Visitors who take the cave tours can sometimes hear low sobbing from the bowels of the cave; others sometimes hear quiet singing.

Another woman is seen in the caves, known as the "Lady in White." She appears either in the caves or at the entrance. When visitors notice her she always fades away quickly.

The former owner and explorer of the caves still watches over the area, making sure guests always find their way back. Frank Schmidt, a resident of Tucson, came to the caves in the early 1920s, and in 1922, he filed two mining claims on the land the cave occupies. In the following year, he opened the cave for tours. The Colossal Cave was quite popular, and in 1934, he gave up rights to the State of Arizona but kept on either giving tours or managing the caves. Frank died a year after he gave up working at the caves at the age of eighty-five.

Today, visitors and tour guides often see Frank hanging around the cave system, usually just watching the guests as they hike along the trails. Some witnesses say he looks just as solid as you or me and others say he is sort of filmy in appearance, but he is always seen as a thin older man wearing a plaid flannel shirt and trousers.

Colossal Cave
East Old Spanish Trail
Vail, AZ 85641
(520) 647-7275
www.colossalcave.com

Douglas

Overloading of the Bisbee smelter caused the Phelps Dodge Corporation with the Calumet and Arizona Copper Company to start new smelters near Douglas. The town site was originally called Black Water, due to the almost undrinkable water found there, but in the years following with the renaming of the town to Douglas, things were cleaned up considerably.

Douglas was one of the last wild west towns where you could still get away with murder. In 1902, the Arizona Rangers were brought in to clean up the town that was tougher than Tombstone.

Gadsden Hotel

In 1907, the Gadsden Hotel opened for business, mainly serving miners, ranchers, and businessmen. The hotel was a masterpiece. The lobby is adorned with a marble staircase, a forty-two-foot Tiffany stained glass mural across the top of the mezzanine, and vaulted stained glass skylights across the lobby area. The marble staircase surrounded by four columns, decorated with fourteen-carat gold on the capital, is estimated to have a value in 1929 of twenty thousand dollars.

Poncho Villa is said to have ridden his horse into the hotel and up the marble staircase while shooting his gun wildly, hollering and causing a commotion. The seventh step of the staircase still has a chip out of it caused by his horse. Unfortunately, you cannot see the bullet holes or any of the other damage he may have caused. Later, the hotel burned down and was rebuilt; the marble staircase survived the fire.

Is Poncho Villa's spirit still riding his horse up the stairs at the Gadsden Hotel?
Courtesy of R.W. O'Brien

Many people claim one of the ghosts haunting the Gadsden Hotel is that of Poncho Villa. One of the ghosts is described as a headless man wearing khaki pants and is seen all over the hotel. He is known to sneak up on guests and tap them on the shoulder or grab their legs. Some guests have heard him whistling an old tune. Is this the spirit of Poncho Villa still trying to get his message across?

Another spirit seen at the hotel is that of a man in western-type clothing lurking in the basement. Is this the spirit who turns lights on and off in the rooms and moves guests' luggage and personal belongings. One guest reported seeing a transparent woman sitting in a chair in the woman's restroom. An Indian boy has been known to play pranks on the mezzanine and Sara, an elderly guest who loved the hotel so much she stayed after death, mainly keeps to the fourth floor.

Gadsden Hotel
1046 G Avenue
Douglas, AZ 85607
(520) 364-4481
www.hotelgadsden.com

Flagstaff

Monte Vista Hotel

Built in 1927, the Monte Vista Hotel was constructed entirely from public taxes. Hoping to provide visitors a place to stay in Flagstaff, the hotel did just that and much more. It soon became home to Mary Costigan's daily three-hour radio show. During prohibition, the hotel became a profitable bootlegging operation, and a gambling hall for about five years with several slot machines located in its lobby. In the 1940s and 1950s, the hotel was home to many famous guests. While filming popular westerns, John Wayne, Gary Cooper, Spencer Tracy, Jane Russell, and Bing Crosby stayed at the Monte Vista. John Wayne even saw one of the hotel's ghosts in his room.

One of the resident ghosts may be one of the men who robbed a bank nearby and stopped in at the hotel for a drink in the 1970s. While robbing the bank one of the three men was shot by the bank guard. Despite his injuries the men made a celebratory stop at the hotel's lounge for a drink. Unfortunately, it was the wounded man's last drink, he bled to death while enjoying it. Guests who shimmy up to the bar will sometimes hear the disembodied voice of the bank robber greeting them with a "Good Morning." Some guests to the bar also complain their drinks move on their own and barstools are rearranged when they come back from the restroom.

Room 306 is home to two prostitutes. During the 1940s, the women were invited up to the room, and during their stay, they were thrown from the balcony to their deaths below. Guests who stay in the room are awakened at night with an intense feeling of being watched and cannot return to sleep. Some guests even report the feeling of a hand covering their mouths or around their throats, cutting off their air supplies.

The Phantom Bellboy is one of the most famous ghosts of the hotel. Late at night, he knocks on room doors and announces "Room Service" but when the guest opens the door, no one is there. John Wayne claimed to have seen the bellboy while he stayed at the hotel in his room. Other guests have also seen the boy outside of room 210.

One past guest of the hotel who seemed to have stayed on is a long time boarder who had an eccentric habit of hanging raw meat from the chandelier in his room. Three days after his death in the 1980s, he was found in room 220. While fixing up the room for the next guests, the repairman experienced the "Meat Man." The repairman left the room briefly to gather more supplies. Upon his return to the room, he found the TV on with full volume and the lights turned back on, the bed linens had been ripped off the bed and scattered around the room.

The most active room in the hotel is room 305, many guests have reported seeing a woman in a rocking chair by the window, and some guests have witnessed the rocking chair moving by itself. An older woman who lived in the room, used to sit in the chair by the window for hours watching the outside world.

The halls of the hotel is where you can find the ghost of a little boy who sometimes will grab your hand or just follow silently behind you. Some of the guests of the hotel claim that he talks but they also think he may be speaking with his mother who may walk with him down the hallways.

Always an eerie experience, a baby's cry is heard from the basement. Mainly the staff has heard the baby, but it is quite frightening to them and they often flee quickly. No one knows who the baby is or what happened, but nonetheless, the baby's cries are loud and disheartening.

The formal lounge is where a ghostly couple are seen, heard laughing, and dancing through the night. The staff and visitors to the hotel have experienced many of these spirits including others that are not so easily named. Shadows dart all over the hotel and objects move without reason all the time. The most frustrating spirit is the one that keeps unscrewing light bulbs, so before you call the front desk about your lights not working, check to see if the bulb is screwed in first; you may be surprised!

Monte Vista Hotel
100 North San Francisco Street
Flagstaff, AZ 86001
(928) 779-6971
www. hotelmontevista.com

Grand Canyon

Where the Colorado River first meets up with the Grand Canyon is where the Hopi Indians emerged from another dimension, entering the Fourth World from the third. It is also, where they access the fifth dimension. Many of the Hopi Indians have psychic abilities and are considered the most spiritual of all the Indian tribes. They are direct descendants of the Anasazi.

Before the Hopi resided in the area, another ancient Indian tribe occupied the area of the Grand Canyon, The Hualapai Indians. They tell the story of how the Grand Canyon was formed. George Wharton James published this account in 1912.

> "The Hualapais say that it was one of their cultural heroes, Pack-i-tha-a-wi, who made the Grand Canyon. There had been a big flood, and the earth was covered with water. No one could stir but Pack-i-tha-a-wi, and he went forth carrying a big knife he had prepared of flint, and a large, heavy, wooden club. He struck the knife deep into the water-covered ground and then smote it deeper and deeper with his club. He moved it back and forth as he struck it further into the earth, until the canyon was formed, through which all the water rushed out into the Sea of the Sunset. Then, as the sun shone, the ground became hard and solid, as we find it to-day."

Many of you may think that it is just a nice Indian legend and the thought that a giant could have actually made the Grand Canyon is preposterous. Although strange, it is very true that in 1896 an explorer to the area discovered gigantic footprints in red sandstone. The footsteps came from a man whose stride was five feet apart. Furthermore, a gigantic petrified body was also discovered in sandstone.

El Tovar Hotel

The El Tovar Hotel was built in 1905 and thought to be the most expensive log cabin in the United States. In its remote locale, it was a luxury to have running hot and cold water, indoor restrooms, electric lights, and of course, its location perched high up on a cliff overlooking the Grand Canyon. The interior was decorated in the rustic theme, walls were adorned with deer, elk, and moose heads, some of which Theodore Roosevelt shot himself. Not much has changed in the hotel over the last hundred years. In 2005, the hotel was updated but you still step into the past as you tread through the lobby doors.

Before you even enter the hotel, you may come upon a ghost. In the middle of the parking lot, in a small patch of grass, is the grave of a former Harvey Girl. The Fred Harvey Company managed the El Tovar from the beginning and staffed the hotel with his famous Harvey Girls. There are several stories floating around who Pirl A. Ward is—the grave marker says her life was from 1879-1934. Most likely, she worked as a Harvey Girl at the El Tovar until her death. Some say she was Fred Harvey's mistress. A few say she was really Mr. Pirl Ward a local rancher and cowboy of the area. I think of her as a Harvey Girl who came out west and found her way to the hotel, happily serving guests their meals in the dining room until her death at the age of fifty-five.

The other mystery about this grave is why she isn't buried at the local cemetery. The Grand Canyon National Park does have a cemetery and it is still in use today. Pirl is still around, most of the sightings place her on the pathway leading from the steps of the El Tovar past her grave and then finally disappearing behind the Hopi House. She is always wearing her Harvey Girl uniform covered in a black hooded cloak.

One visitor to the hotel claimed, after placing some flowers on the much forgotten grave, he had several strokes of good luck and claims it was Pirl looking out for him. First, after trying to stay at the hotel for years, a room suddenly became available in his price range. The night was wonderful and he had a great experience. After leaving the hotel, his Toyota Camry hit what the park rangers describe as the largest buck they have seen. Although the deer was fatally hit and flew across the road into a ditch, the Camry sustained little damage, just a cracked headlight, a few small dents, and a broken windshield. It was very lucky the car was not totaled and no one was hurt. If you have traveled, then you know how hard it is to get repairs done away from home, especially in a remote area. Not this Friday night! A shop in Flagstaff happened to have one windshield and it was the exact match for the Camry; if that wasn't enough, the garage came out and replaced the windshield that night. Pirl must have been looking out for the kind-hearted man that left her the flowers.

Another spirit at the El Tovar is Fred Harvey himself. He appears on the third floor, especially around the holiday season inviting travelers to the many festivities at the hotel. He is always observed wearing a hat and long coat. Many other reports place him in the kitchen and dining rooms, surely making sure things are going smoothly, and the guests are happy.

As many as fourteen spirits haunt the El Tovar, besides Fred Harvey and Pril there are two little boys who knock over merchandise in the gift shop. Big balls of light have been seen floating around the hotel and guests have quickly checked out of their rooms in the middle of the night, frightened by spirits in their rooms.

El Tovar Hotel
West Rim Drive
Grand Canyon Village, AZ 86023
(303) 297-2757
www.grandcanyonlodges.com

Jerome

Built on a steep hillside, Jerome, Arizona, has always been mined for its copper and silver. Native Americans were interested in the copper for its pigment and Spaniards mined the hills for silver when the land was part of New Spain. In 1883, Cleopatra Hill was settled as a mining camp. After much urging from his wife, Eugene Jerome purchased the mineral rights to the land and financed the first mines. Over the next seventy years, the United

Verde Mine produced an astounding one billion dollars in copper, silver, and even gold. The men that mined Jerome helped it gain the reputation as "the wickedest town in the west."

During its heyday, Jerome was the fourth largest city in Arizona, supporting more than 15,000 copper mines, brothels, saloons, and opium dens. Like all hastily built mining boomtowns, fire was always a concern. After the 1899 fire, the town of Jerome was rebuilt out of brick and masonry. In 1918, another fire struck, this time in the mines. Fires consumed twenty-two miles of the underground mines, one of the mines burned for twenty years prompting the closing of underground mines and moving the operations to the open-pit style.

In 1935, the Phelps Dodge Company bought the Douglas Mine and started blasting away at the mountain side. The Phelps Dodge Company would ignite up to 250,000 pounds of dynamite at a time, causing many of the towns' buildings to slide down the hill due to its steep location. On one occasion, the jail slid down the hill and came to a stop intact a block below its original location. Today the jail is a tourist attraction known as the "Sliding Jail." Other buildings that slid down the towns' hillside were a movie theater, JC Penny's, and a pool hall. Some of the businesses in Jerome just crumpled due to the shaking the dynamite created.

The year 1952 saw the end of the Dodge Phelps Mining Company in Jerome. The miners had no union and no other employment in the town. Soon, the town, which at its boom saw as many as 15,000 people, was struggling to maintain 50 families. The town remained quiet until the late 1960s when a new generation moved in and awoke the spirits of the past.

Mile High Grill & Inn

The building that houses the Mile High Grill & Inn was originally built in 1899 and known as the Clinksdale Building. The building has housed apartments, a hardware store, and a morgue before turning into a restaurant and inn in the 1990s.

Jennie Banters, who was one of the towns madams running her bordello from the premises, is said to still walk around at the inn. Jennie was, at one time, one of the richest women in Arizona. In an attempt to clean up the town, the bordellos were moved away from the Main Street to "Husbands Alley." This is where Jennie lost her life to one of her clients like many of the prostitutes of the time. Jennie, an older gentleman, and a phantom cat have all been reported at the Mile High Inn.

The cat is thought to be Jennie's, brushing up against guests' legs and leaving footprints on freshly made beds. Some guests even have seen the phantom feline walking down the hall and have heard his meow late at night while scratching at the door to be let out. Luckily, the cat can just walk through the door when it wants out.

Jennie is thought to move objects in the guest rooms flinging them across the room when not satisfied. One story recounts a vase in the Victorian Rose room, which flew across the room crashing to the floor nearly missing the housekeeper, who just finished making up the room. The vase was replaced and about a year later took flight again. Is Jennie asking for different flowers or just does she just want some attention?

A brass cherub at the top of the stairs at the Mile High Grill & Inn has been known to spin around when no one is near, and there has been the smell of perfume wafting through the hallway. Other phenomena include the doors opening on their own after guests have locked them and turned in for the night. As they lay in bed, the door will open, and then after a minute or two, close and relock.

Several guests have also reported experiencing a strong cold wind in the Memories of the Heart room. In the Lariat and Lace room, housekeeping claims the spirit that resides there insists the room is cleaned first. They comply knowing the mess that will follow if they start with another room first.

Ghostly fingers spin a cherub statue at the Mile High Grill and Inn. *Courtesy of R.W. O'Brien*

All the rooms have ghostly stories attached to them at the Mile High Grill & Inn including the restaurant where glasses break and containers fall off shelves. Employees and guests have reported hearing whistling and unearthly voices all over the building.

Mile High Grill & Inn
309 Main Street
Jerome, AZ 86331
(928) 634-5094
www.jeromemilehighinn.com

Connor Hotel

David Connor built the first-class Connor Hotel in 1897. At the spendy price of a dollar per night, the hotel offered twenty rooms with a bar and billiards on the first floor. After being destroyed by two fires, Connor rebuilt the elegant hotel one last time from insurance money he received in 1899. Connor even offered a bus to and from the train depot for guests. Unfortunately, in 1931, the hotel closed due to the dwindling mining economy. The Connor Hotel was still used for small shops downstairs with the upstairs rooms sitting empty.

After the mines finally closed in the 1950s, the town became virtually a ghost town. In the following decades, the town experienced resurgence with tourists and artists moving in. The hotel opened again, but not with the original grandeur it once had. After closing in the 1980s for a much needed remodel, the hotel once again rose up and now shows itself as the jewel it was once.

The Connor Hotel has several rooms that are reportedly haunted. One well-worn story is that of an electrician who attempted to stay the night in room number 1. Sometime during the night someone or something laid down with him in bed; he was so terrified that he spent the rest of the night in his van. On other occasions, guests have heard whispers and women laughing in the room. Ghost hunters have investigated this room and have reported witnessing the armoire doors opening on their own.

Right:
An electrician fled after having a presence lay in bed with him at the Connor Hotel. *Courtesy of R.W. O'Brien*

Room number 2 has the most activity according to the innkeeper. Objects that guests have left out have mysteriously gone missing and then reappear later in a different spot, especially if left in the bathroom. A barking dog has been heard in room number 4 as well as an elderly man coughing. Employees and guests from the hallway outside the room have heard all of this. A local to the area has seen David Connor and a prostitute from the era enter the hotel on one occasion.

Connor Hotel
164 Main Street
Jerome, AZ 86331
(928) 634-5006
www.connorhotel.com

Jerome Grand Hotel

In 1927, the United Verde Copper Company built the United Verde Hospital to serve the citizens of Jerome, who were mainly mine employees and their families. It turned out to be a 30,000-square-foot show place perched high above Jerome on Cleopatra Hill as well as the last major structure built in Jerome. The hospital was closed in 1950 due to the decline of the mining business and the lack of population in Jerome. For the next forty-four years the great hospital stood silently, waiting for its doors to reopen once again. In 1994, the building was resurrected once again into the gleaming Jerome Grand Hotel it is now.

Reports of ghosts started with the patients of the hospital. Patients claimed to see a phantom nurse standing on the balcony and many would claim to hear disembodied voices, coughing, crying, and the moans of pain. Speculation at the time thought the souls who died from the 1917 flu epidemic somehow found their way to the hotel. One spirit that has been seen from the first days of the hospital is that of a bearded miner. A hospital patient first reported the miner gliding down the hallway, lights flickering on as he passed by them. Later a nurse reported seeing him at the end of a hallway, and as she approached, he disappeared. Guests of the hotel today still see the miner in the hallways.

Sick patients still call the Jerome Grand Hotel home even after death. *Courtesy of R.W. O'Brien*

The Jerome Grand Hotel is so popular with ghosts and tourists looking for ghosts that it offers ghost tours and has a web page dedicated to the ghosts of the hotel. Nevertheless, you don't need to stay at the hotel to have a ghostly experience. The Asylum Restaurant located in the old hospital asylum has had its share of ghostly experiences. One patron to the restaurant could not shake the feeling of being watched and another saw the faint image of a little boy running through the bar area.

Staff at the hotel have their own unique challenges mostly in part from the ghostly residents. Staff in the lobby have to contend with the front doors opening and closing as the departed souls come and go, as well as the lobby seating being rearranged when the employees are looking in the opposite direction. The front desk often receives calls from vacant locked rooms, and in the gift shop area, merchandise flies off shelves daily. The housekeeping staff has to contend with hearing their names called out when no one is around. Electronics turn on and off and cleaning supplies move or come up missing. One member of the housekeeping staff even witnessed a spirit moving down the third floor hallway and others have witnessed a nurse carrying a clipboard still doing her rounds.

A few guests of the hotel complain that after enjoying a meal in the restaurant and upon returning to their room, all of their personal belongings are packed back in their suitcases. Other guests have reported someone knocking on their doors at night. When the guest answers no one is there but they hear footsteps walking away down the hall. Many of the guests who have taken the ghost tour of the hotel have taken photos that revealed anomalies.

A 1926 Otis elevator is still taking guests to their rooms. Many are unaware of the ghost and the "accident" that surrounds this original elevator. Claude Harvey was the maintenance man in 1935 for the hospital.

Jerome Grand Hotel's Otis elevator still runs even without an operator working the switch.
Courtesy of R.W.O'Brien

He was found dead under the elevator; the inquest into his death revealed the elevator did not kill him. Was he murdered and placed under the elevator or maybe he committed suicide? The official reports conclude his death was an accident. Since Harvey's death, strange balls of light have appeared in the elevator shaft. Employees claim to have seen a shadowy man in the basement and around the elevator. Is this Harvey trying to point to his murderer?

Other spirits who had untimely deaths at the hotel include a wheelchair-bound man pulling himself up and over the balcony, ultimately falling to his death, a caretaker of the once-vacant hospital who hanged himself, and a woman who died in childbirth who is still looking for her dead baby's body after the hospital staff buried it in an unmarked grave.

Being a former hospital, one would expect some paranormal activity. Many patients were treated and sent on their way while a great number of others perished within the hospital walls. Women came to have their babies in the third floor maternity ward; some died as well as some of the babies. The emergency room, which is where the lobby is now located, saw much blood and trauma. The third floor is where surgeries took place and no one knows for sure how many perished while being attended on the surgery table. Others just came to die at the hospital and many remain.

Jerome Grand Hotel
200 Hill Street
Jerome, AZ 86331
(928) 634-8200
www.jeromegrandhotel.com

Nogales

St. Andrew's Episcopal Church

Built on the border of Mexico, Nogales is a bustling town founded in 1893, with one side in Mexico and the other side in Arizona. St. Andrew's Episcopal Church was founded in Tombstone in 1899; later the congregation moved to Nogales where the church found its home in 1908 in sleepy border town of Nogales. The church stayed at that location until 1968 when the Interstate was slated to go right through the church. In November 1970, a new St. Andrew's Episcopal Church was constructed across town. Many of the original items from the previous church, including the stained glass windows, were saved and installed in the new church.

Immediately, the church felt like home to its congregation which included a few new worshipers. It appears ancient Indians visit the church, a whole tribe has been witnessed in the front pews of St. Andrew's during an organ practice. An older man wrapped in an old native blanket appears quite often all over the church. He has been seen by priests and parishioners alike, appearing suddenly and then quietly fading away.

It was not until maintenance work was being done on the plumbing that ancient Indian bones and an urn were discovered under the modern church. The ancient Indians must be at peace with the new addition to their burial ground, or are they?

St. Andrew's Episcopal Church
969 West Country Club Drive
Nogales, AZ 85621
520-281-1523
www.standrewsaz.org

Prescott

Hotel Vendome

The Hotel Vendome was built in 1917 by rancher Jack Jones who came to Prescott, Arizona, for a new start. In the early 1900s, Prescott had an urgent need for places to live and the Hotel Vendome filled that need with thirty modern apartment-type rooms. The rooms included hot and cold water, steam heat, and phone service with buzzers. One famous cowboy actor, Tom Mix, rented a room by the year.

Jones hired a manager to run the hotel and soon moved on to something more challenging, driving a delivery truck. By 1924, Jones decided he'd had enough, sold the hotel, and went back to ranching.

Abby Byr came to Prescott with her husband to find relief for tuberculosis. They bought the hotel but soon lost it due to unpaid taxes. The new owners felt bad for the couple and let them stay on in room 16. Soon after, Abby's husband deserted his wife, leaving her alone at the hotel with her beloved cat. Devastated, Abby refused to eat or drink and starved to death with her cat in 1925.

Today, Abby and her cat still hang around room 16 at Hotel Vendome. The TV in her room turns on and off by itself. Guests have reported the radiator will switch on after they turn it off, and some even report they have heard meowing when no cats are around.

Hotel Vendome
230 South Cortez Street
Prescott, AZ 86303
(928) 776-0900
www.vendomehotel.com

Superstition Mountains

The Superstition Mountains lie just east of Phoenix, Arizona. The range is about forty miles long and fifteen miles wide, with the peak reaching over 4,500 feet. Many of its mountains go straight up and are nearly impossible to climb, even though prospectors and explorers have been scaling the mountains since they were first discovered.

All the lore first started when the Spanish arrived in 1540 with Coronado. The local Indians told the Spanish the mountains were full of gold and the Thunder god protected the mountains. The Thunder god would kill all who set foot on his sacred land. The Spanish ignored this warning and continued with their search for gold. Funny thing happened, the group of men were fine as long as they were together but as soon as one would stray from the group, he would disappear. When the group later found him, the body would be mutilated and decapitated. This happened to a few men before Coronado decided it was too dangerous and left the mountain. He named the mountain Monte Superstition.

Death and Mystery surrounds the Superstition Mountains.
Courtesy of BigStockPhoto

The next settlers to enter the mountain range was in the late 1800s. Jacob Waltz of the Lost Dutchmen Mine fame mined the mountains. He was unharmed, but his partner, Jacob Weiser, came up missing. Some locals speculated Waltz killed him or the local Apaches captured him, but others thought it was the mountain. Many more prospectors came to the mountains and many more went missing over the years. It seems the Indians knew something about the mountains; supernatural forces appeared to be at work.

The Lost Dutchman Mine

There are so many stories about the Lost Dutchman Mine, the following is a brief version. Around 1860, Jacob Waltz purchased a mining claim in the Superstition Mountains. By 1889, Waltz was eighty years old and had pulled forty-eight pounds of gold from his mine; he apparently kept his cache under his bed. When he fell sick, he was taken care of by his friend, Julia Thomas. For her kindness, Waltz gave her the instructions for finding his secret mine in the mountains. He claimed the veins of gold were fourteen inches thick.

Julia and her father spent the rest of their lives looking for this mine; the directions to the mine were vague at best.

> "To get to the mine, you have to crawl through a hole. You can see the Old Military Trail from the mine, but you cannot see it from the mine trail. You can see Weavers Needle in the Superstitions by climbing up a short distance. The sun sets on the gold in my mine. There is a face looking up at my mine."

Ever since, prospectors and treasure hunters have been risking their lives in the Superstition Mountains looking for the Lost Dutchman's Mine.

In the late 1880s, two soldiers made their way to Pinal, Arizona, looking for work at the Silver King Mine. The manager of the mine, Aaron Mason, was more interested in the bag of gold ore the two men carried with them. The men explained that while crossing the Superstition Mountains they came across an old mine. Mason bought the ore from them and entered into a partnership with the men. The two men were sure they could find the mine again but after a few weeks they had not returned and Mason sent out a search party. Their bodies were found, nude shot in the head.

Another prospector, Elisha Marcus Reavis, was known as the Madman of the Superstitions, or Old Hermit because he never shaved, cut his hair or bathed. There was also talk he would run naked through the canyons firing a pistol in the sky. He may have been mad as even the Apache left him alone. After a few weeks, his friends went looking for him. His body was found several feet away from his head.

In 1910, a skeleton of a woman was found in a cave high up on the mountain range. Several gold nuggets were found near her body. In 1927, a New Jersey man and his sons were hiking in the mountains when rocks began to tumble onto their trail as if someone were pushing them deliberately from above. One of the boy's leg was crushed. The next year two hunters were driven off the road when boulders were mysteriously "pushed" from above.

In 1931, Adolph Ruth, a treasure hunter from Washington, D.C. went missing. He was well equipped and had acquired a treasure map of the mines in the Superstition Mountains. Two local cowboys packed Ruth into the mountains. When there was no sign of him a week later, the cowboys went looking for him. Tex Barkley arrived at Ruth's camp and found that Ruth had not been there in at least a day. He then issued a reward. Forty-five days passed and no one could find any sign of Ruth, all hope was lost and the search was given up. That winter a skull with two bullet holes was found and it turned out to be

Adolph Ruth's skull. The following month his body was discovered and the map was nowhere to be found.

In 1937, prospector Guy Frink actually returned from the mountain with a small fortune of gold ore. A few months later his body was found shot on a trail leading into the mountains, a small fortune in ore stacked neatly beside him.

James Cravey searched for the Lost Dutchman mine by helicopter, the pilot set him down close to Weavers Needle; when Cravey failed to hike out of the mountains, a search was performed. His camp was found and it was not until the next spring that his headless corpse was found with a blanket tied around it. His skull was found in a canyon. The coroner could find no evidence of foul play.

The 1950s produced one mysterious death after the next. Each year at least one man died or disappeared. The 1960s produced a lot of the skeletons from the lost prospectors. A group of hikers found the skeleton of Franz Harrier and five days later another skeleton was found of a painter from San Francisco. The following year a family picnicking found the body of Hilmer Charles Bohen, he was shot in the back and buried in some sand. Two months later another body was found riddled with bullets, the coroner ruled it a suicide. I could go on through the decades up to current but it is the same story.

If you are foolish enough to go to the Superstition Mountain Range, BEWARE. Besides the obvious curse the mountains hold, some of the survivors to the mountain makes claims of seeing strange lights dance around and others wonder who really is pushing the boulders onto them. Apaches left the mountains long ago; legends state there were too many spirits in the range. No one knows what mysteries this mountain range really holds.

Tombstone

We all know the town from the famous fight at the OK Corral. We have seen the movies about Wyatt Earp and Doc Holliday. The town is still there and so are many of the buildings that existed during the time. With all the history, there is no wonder many visitors and residents to the town of Tombstone report experiencing the spirits who remain there.

The Earps came to Tombstone to settle down, mine, and run a saloon. They found much more than a peaceful town in which to grow roots. Virgil Earp decided to become deputy marshal and his brother, Morgan, also joined up. Before long Wyatt had become involved again with the law as he joined his two brothers. The Cowboys gang who were known for robbing stagecoaches, rustling cattle, and disturbing the peace in Tombstone became public enemy number one when a particularly unsavory member of the gang shot the unsuspecting Marshal Fred White. Curly Bill Brocius unknowingly lit the fuse that would explode into the famous OK Corral fight between the Earps and the Cowboys. Marshal Fred White was murdered in the lot that would hold the future Birdcage Theater.

The Bird Cage

This was not the last murder that would happen at the Bird Cage. From the beginning, the Bird Cage was known as the roughest nightspot on the West Coast. Open twenty-four hours a day for nine years, the Bird Cage was witness to twenty-six men and one woman being killed from sixteen gunfights. You can still see the one hundred-forty bullet holes in the walls of the building. The building is named for the fourteen Bird Cage Cribs that overhang the casino and dance hall area.

Under the dance hall and stage is a room where the longest poker game in history occurred, lasting continually for eight years, five months, and three days. The poker game involved such heavy weights as Adolph Busch and George Hearst as well as more seasoned gamblers such as Bat Masterson and Doc Holliday. A minimum of one thousand dollars was required to enter the game. You can still see the table today as well as the table Doc Holliday ran his Faro game on. Downstairs also holds a room known as Josephine's Room. This is where Wyatt Earp and his third wife Josephine "Sadie" Marcus first had relations together.

Outlaws, miners, and prostitutes are still partying the night away at the Bird Cage Theater. *Courtesy of R.W. O'Brien*

In 1889, the Bird Cage closed after the mines flooded, causing the miners to move to Bisbee. After years of being boarded up, the building was reopened in 1934 and was preserved in its original state. The Bird Cage also holds many other artifacts from the town including a hearse, which is trimmed in twenty-four carat gold and silver. The Black Moriah cost eight thousand dollars in the late 1800s and took most of the deceased from Tombstone to Boothill. The current value of the Black Moriah is two million dollars.

With all the history and death packed into such a small building, it's no wonder more than a few spirits call the Bird Cage home. The first reports of ghostly shenanigans started back in 1921 when a school was built across the street. Students started reporting hearing laughter and music emanating from the derelict building. One resident in the apartments above the Silver Nugget claims to have seen, early one morning, the spirits of gunslingers, miners, and cattlemen pour out of the Bird Cage into the street in front of him, perhaps from a long night of partying.

Many of the staff and visitors have reported seeing apparitions inside the building. The apparition most often reported is of a stagehand wearing a visor and black stripped pants holding a clipboard and walking across the stage. Another apparition sighted frequently is of a woman wearing a white dress from the 1800s era. Many other reports of strange occurrences include objects moving or disappearing only to reappear later. Also in the Bird Cage the smell of cigar smoke and of perfume float through the rooms. Even more common are reports of hearing old-time music and strange sounds coming from the balconies, some even report hearing clinking glasses and cards shuffling.

Bird Cage Theater
517 East Allen Street
Tombstone, AZ 85638
(800) 457-3423
tombstonebirdcage.com

Boothill Cemetery

Just the name Boothill conjures up thoughts of withered wooden crosses emerging from rock mounds, overgrown and overrun with mice, snakes, and ghosts, and don't forget the dead tree that still stands. Many photos surface with the mist or a stream of light that cannot be explained away in this graveyard. Some lucky visitors have taken a photo or two with a full-blown apparition appearing in it. It is no wonder so many people have experiences in this cemetery. More than 250 souls are buried in the graveyard, many of which did not choose to die. Some were hanged, one by mistake. Some died from gunfights, including the victims of the OK Corral fight. Some were killed by their lovers or while they were trying to keep a love. Prostitutes, outlaws, miners, lawmen, and even children are all buried in Tombstone's cemetery.

Are these the men who roam the grounds of Boothill? *Courtesy of R.W. O'Brien*

Originally called the Tombstone Cemetery, it wasn't until 1929 when, after years of abandonment, the cemetery was rediscovered and renamed Boothill Graveyard (for tourists I'm sure). It was not until the 1940s when the town started the cleanup and restoration of the grounds and replaced stolen or lost markers. Today, the cemetery is one of the most visited sites in Tombstone. Visitors have reported seeing lights hovering and hearing unexplained noises coming from the grounds. A popular tale states Billy Clanton, who was killed in the fight at the OK Corral, rises from his grave and walks back to Tombstone along the road.

Boothill Cemetery
408 North Hwy 80
Tombstone, AZ 85638
(520) 457-3300
www.boothillgiftshop.com

Big Nose Kate's Saloon and the Grand Hotel

Before the great fire of 1882, Big Nose Kate's Saloon was the Grand Hotel. Opening in 1880, the lavish hotel offered guests sixteen rooms with a view. The lobby held three chandeliers and the furniture was walnut laid upon plush carpet and even hot and cold running water. On September 9th, 1880, an invitation-only ball was held at the hotel as a grand opening celebration. With such fine accommodations, it is no wonder such big names stayed at the hotel. Wyatt and his brother Virgil Earp have stayed at the hotel as well as Doc Holliday; Ike Clanton and the McLaury brothers stayed at the hotel the night before the OK Corral gunfight.

In the basement of the Grand Hotel lived a janitor many called the "Swamper." While his day job was keeping the hotel in great shape, he had a sideline in the basement. Below the hotel, Swamper had a mine shaft; no one knows for sure what he did with all the silver he discovered under the hotel—some say it is still hidden in the mine shafts or in the basement where his room was.

The fire of 1882 destroyed the Grand Hotel. After burning down, another structure was built that now houses Big Nose Kate's Saloon. Even though the original hotel is gone, the basement where Swamper lived and dug out his mine still remains. Employees and patrons to the Saloon claim that Swamper remains as well. Is he protecting his silver or looking for it? Many reports claim Swamper roams the halls and appears in photos.

Does a ghost protect his hidden treasure at Big Nose Kates Saloon.
Courtesy of R.W.O'Brien

Other spirits appeared in the saloon, too. A group of cowboys are seen hanging around the bar area. The bar from the Grand Hotel survived the fire and is still used in the present day saloon. Lights have been reported turning on and off, doors open and close and objects fall off shelves and display cases. If that's not creepy enough, mannequins in the building move by themselves. Voices and footsteps are heard throughout the building.

Big Nose Kate's Saloon
417 East Allen Street
Tombstone, AZ 85638
520.457.3107
www.bignosekates.info

Crystal Palace Saloon

Built after the second Tombstone fire, the Crystal Palace Saloon was the complete opposite of the Bird Cage Opera House and Saloon. With its fine crystal glasses and its clean gambling games, the Saloon was a favorite among the more prominent citizens of Tombstone. One of the reasons the saloon stayed clean and respectable was the offices of the marshal, and the towns coroner were upstairs above the saloon.

As the town dried up, so did the saloon; in 1963, the Crystal Palace Saloon was purchased by a restoration group, and after many years, was brought back to life with its former elegance, restored inch by inch from historical photographs.

Crystal Palace is where the ghosts of gamblers never stopped playing roulette.
Courtesy of R.W. O'Brien

Once a favorite of Doc Holliday's girlfriend, Big Nose Kate, it seems that Kate still sticks around long after death. Employees report hearing voices and footsteps late at night. When the building is empty, an unseen dealer turns the gambling wheels of the roulette table. Visitors outside the building have seen cowboys inside the building sidling up to the bar and playing games at the tables.

Crystal Palace Saloon and Restaurant
436 East Allen Street
Tombstone, AZ 85638
(520) 457-3611
www.crystalpalacesaloon.com

OK Corral

When most people think of Tombstone, they think of the OK Corral, Wyatt Earp, Doc Holliday, and the Cowboys. They may have preconceived notions of what happened during the famous gunfight from television shows or movies on the subject; many of the facts have been glorified and twisted to make a better story. Yes, a gunfight did happen and you can go see where it happened and find out all the details. But with any story as famous as the gunfight at the OK Corral, things are not exactly as they were in Tombstone's heyday. The OK Corral is now a tourist stop, not a place to keep your horses. Walls have gone up and you can buy a souvenir keychain or a t-shirt to remember your visit.

The OK Corral reportedly is haunted. Ghost hunters have stated hearing music from the turn of the century and voices as well as footsteps on the boardwalk and in the gift shop area. Visitors to the site claim to have seen the ghosts of the Earps and McLaurys with their guns drawn. Many employees and patrons to the site have reported seeing a bearded man known to the area as James Burnett. James was in a dispute with a neighbor of his, William Greene, over water, which ended up causing Greene's daughter's death. Greene shot Burnett while he was sitting at the OK Corral and was later found not guilty of the murder.

According to newspaper accounts following the great gunfight at the OK Corral, Marshal Earp and his brothers with Doc Holliday met up with the Cowboys (the Clantons and the McLaurys) in the alleyway by the OK Corral. The Earps asked the Cowboys to throw up their hands to disarm the group. The Earps may have been looking for a fight as much as the Cowboys were. The two groups had several different grievances for quite some time and some sort of confrontation was inevitable. In less than thirty seconds, Billy Clanton, Tom McLaury, and his brother were fatally shot. Marshal Virgil Earp was shot in the right leg and his brother Morgan was shot in both shoulders. The gun ball entered Morgan's right shoulder passed through his back shattering a piece of vertebrae then exiting the through the left shoulder. Doc Holliday had just been grazed and as a result walked with a limp. Wyatt Earp was the only member of the gunfight to come out without harm.

Many think of the gunfight as the end of the dispute between the groups, but I always think of it as the beginning of years of fighting. The survivors then executed revenge on the Earps, killing Morgan Earp with snipers, a shot while he played pool, and Virgil Earp was shot in the arm. Wyatt Earp sent his remaining family and their wives to California. Wyatt and Doc Holliday then spent the next few years killing anyone who may have been involved with the Cowboys or the killing of his brother, Morgan. As a result of all the animosity and killings, many of the victims still haunt the site of the famous gunfight or where they were later shot down.

Wyatt Earp gathered up several men and went on a killing spree. The first man down was Frank Stilwell. He was found the morning after Wyatt Earp and his posse loaded what remained of his family, and his brother's coffin onto a train headed for Colton, California, where his parents resided. Stilwell was reportedly found in the rail yard with one witness claiming he heard ten gunshots the night before and then some cheering. The coroner's inquest found five bullet holes in Stilwell, one for each member of Earp's posse. Then the posse rode out of Tombstone and found Florentino, and opened fire. Florentino's death brought on another posse to stop Earp and his men from killing any more men. This posse, lead by the now appointed sheriff of Tombstone, John Behan, included men from the Cowboys as well as Johnny Ringo and Fin Clanton. The Earp posse came upon Iron Springs, thinking Charlie Smith was hiding out there; instead of Smith, a group of Cowboys were waiting to ambush the Earp posse and opened fire without warning. After a barrage of gunfire, the Earp posse walked away with only the loss of a horse. When Wyatt emerged, he had taken down one of the main players of the Cowboys, Curly Bill Brocius. Much speculation followed if Wyatt's story about Curly Bill's death was true, but Curly Bill never was seen again. Wyatt was just about done with his vendetta and headed to New Mexico, then on to Colorado.

The remaining Cowboys that Wyatt did not catch up with met their fate. Johnny Ringo was found dead—some say that Doc Holliday caught up to him—and Ike Clanton was shot after resisting arrest.

Johnny Ringo's grave can still be seen beside Turkey Creek. Ringo was buried where his body had been found, a bullet hole in his forehead. The coroner ruled his death a suicide. No one really knows what happened, but Ringo's spirit is still seen around Turkey Creek and in the crook of the tree where his lifeless body was found.

OK Corral

308 East Allen Street
Tombstone, AZ 85638
(520) 457-3456
www.ok-corral.com

Tucson

Velasco Pueblo

Built in the 1850s, the Velasco Pueblo has three main rooms in the original structure. Carlos Velasco bought the house in 1878 and several other rooms were added. Carlos Velasco was a Sonoran State Senator, district judge, general store owner and started a Spanish newspaper, *El Fronterizo*, right from his home until his death in 1914.

The house stood abandoned until it was bought by Charles Brown, Bill Dillon, and William Cobb. The three men took to restoring the house, replacing the termite-eaten floors and timber beams that crossed the ceilings. A fire had blackened one room where Velasco's printing press had once been. It was not long after they started working on the house they had their first brush with the unexplained.

While working in the bedroom that led to the printing room, Brown noticed the upper torso of a man watching him doing his work. After reviewing some photos, Brown identified Carlos Velasco as the man he saw. Since the initial sighting, others have come to see Carlos in different parts of the house just silently observing. Carlos is also blamed for resetting the time on clocks around the house, and rearranging furniture when the house is unoccupied.

Vulture Mine

In 1863, an immigrant from Austria discovered gold near the White Quarts Butte. One of the more colorful stories about Henry Wickenburg's gold discovery was that he shot a vulture and its body happened to land on a gold nugget, which lead to the Vulture Mine. The mine began to produce enough gold to substantiate the claim to be one of the richest mines in Arizona. Unfortunately, it never paid out to its many investors, including Henry Wickenburg, who died penniless from a self-inflicted gunshot to the head.

Glory Hole

At the Glory Hole (a pit that originated in 1923) seven miners and twelve burros died from a cave-in after the support pillars were compromised. All the bodies are still in the hole never to be recovered. Are these some of the men who, long after death, still frequent some of the old, abandoned stores and buildings at the Vulture Mine town site in Arizona?

Hanging Tree

Eighteen residents died at the end of a rope attached to the hanging tree. The spirits of some are said to still roam the area looking for their next victim or looking for some real justice having been unlawfully accused of the crime they died for.

Ghostly Children

A diphtheria outbreak took the lives of around one hundred and twenty of the children who lived in or near the town. Small mounds are the only remains of the graves; many years ago the original grave markers were stolen. A ghostly young boy has been seen near the cemetery keeping watch over his friends' graves. Many visitors who have taken photos in the area report having a blue orb show up in the photos.

Mess Hall

A former resident of the town claims hearing ghostly knocking, voices, footsteps and shadows in the dusty buildings of the town. The mess hall is the site of many ghostly experiences. Bread and stew smells waft through the building from the kitchen. Many visitors have also reported hearing silverware clinking against dishes and the sounds of chairs scraping against the floor with no such movement in sight.

Assay House

The Assay Office for the Vulture Mine was constructed in 1884, primarily out of ore from the mine. The walls contain over six hundred thousand dollars in silver and gold. The building is well known for its paranormal activity. Electronic Voice Phenomena has turned up much evidence that something or someone still remains from the Vulture Mine's glorious past.

Yuma

Yuma Territorial Prison

Many men were tormented and died inside the Yuma Territorial Prison which inmates built themselves. In 1876, seven inmates working on the prison were locked in the cells they shared with scorpions and rattlesnakes. For a little extra torture, the guards dropped many of these deadly creatures into the cells with the inmates. Among the prisoners who served their time at the prison over its thirty-three years in service were twenty-nine women. One hundred and ten men and one woman died behind the walls of the prison. Many of the deaths were from a tuberculosis outbreak, a few committed suicide and a total of twenty-six men escaped into the Yuma desert. Eight men died trying to escape, and one man escaped by vanishing into a rock.

How did one prisoner vanish from Yuma Territorial Prison?
Courtesy of BigStockPhoto

Two famous inmates, Pearl Hart and John Bowen spent some time at Yuma. Pearl Hart was one of the last stagecoach robbers. She was known to wear tight men's pants, smoked, drank, and used other drugs of the time. On May 30, 1899, Pearl and John robbed the stagecoach that ran between Florence and Globe, Arizona. The pair rode off with $450 from the heist, but they soon got lost in the surrounding desert. After making camp for the night in a groove of trees, the couple woke to a posse surrounding them. Pearl was tried and found not guilty by a jury that she swayed by flirting with. The judge was furious and retried her for unlawfully carrying a gun, this time she was found guilty and shipped off to Yuma Territorial Prison. John was tried separately and had no luck with the jury; he was sentenced to thirty years for the robbery.

Pearl had a friendship with the warden who allowed her some luxuries, a larger cell, gentlemen callers and a few other niceties to make her stay more comfortable. She was paroled in 1902. Pearl would surface several times over the years, usually for smaller crimes, and eventually faded away into history.

John was another story all together. He was well spoken and a model prisoner; in fact, he was so good that one morning he missed breakfast and no one noticed. He was just under two years at the prison, when he vanished. One prisoner claimed to have seen him the prior day at the granite bluff. John was facing the bluff with his palms towards the rock, making a humming sound, then without a word he stepped forward and vanished. The man who witnessed this made his way over to the rock and tried to escape through the rock as John Bowen had, but he quickly found it was a solid rock!

When John and Pearl were lost in the desert they camped next to Poston's Butte. The butte is of particular interest because Charles Poston spent some time in India and upon returning to the states turned the butte into a temple to the sun. In 1939, an American named Elijah Bowen was traveling through India looking for the Hidden Masters. Elijah was from Ashburnham, Massachusetts, the same as John Bowen. Was this the same man? Did he discover something magical in Poston's Butte that allowed him to vanish from the prison?

The prison closed its doors to inmates but opened them up for the homeless during the depression. Many people called the small cells their homes during this hard time.

Many spirits remain at the prison including one depression era little girl who drowned trying to rescue her doll from the Colorado River. She is seen dressed in red and must like the color as she plays with any red clothing visitors wear to the grounds. Other spirits that remain within the crumbling prison include a superintendent who committed suicide by pressing a gun to his temple and firing.

The Dark Cell or Snake Pit is a hole in the wall, literally, hand carved out of a granite hillside with only a six inch air hole. It served as a time out for the inmates who just couldn't behave. Many of the prisoners went insane when put in there and two went directly to an asylum after their stay in the Dark Cell. Many of them are still in there today. Visitors and park employees have witnessed malevolent human shaped shadows in and near the cell, one employee talks of feeling a presence in the cell that frightened her.

Many of the prisoners who are doomed to stay incarcerated are just happy to open and close doors. One reporter got mysteriously locked in a cell as she was doing a news broadcast, lights turn on and off and change from the cash register have been known to fly out. The heavy ball and chain that was fastened to the prisoner's leg can still be heard clanking and dragging on the ground as these spirits still go about their business.

Yuma Territorial Prison
1 Prison Hill Road
Yuma, AZ 85364
(928) 783-4771
www.pr.state.az.us

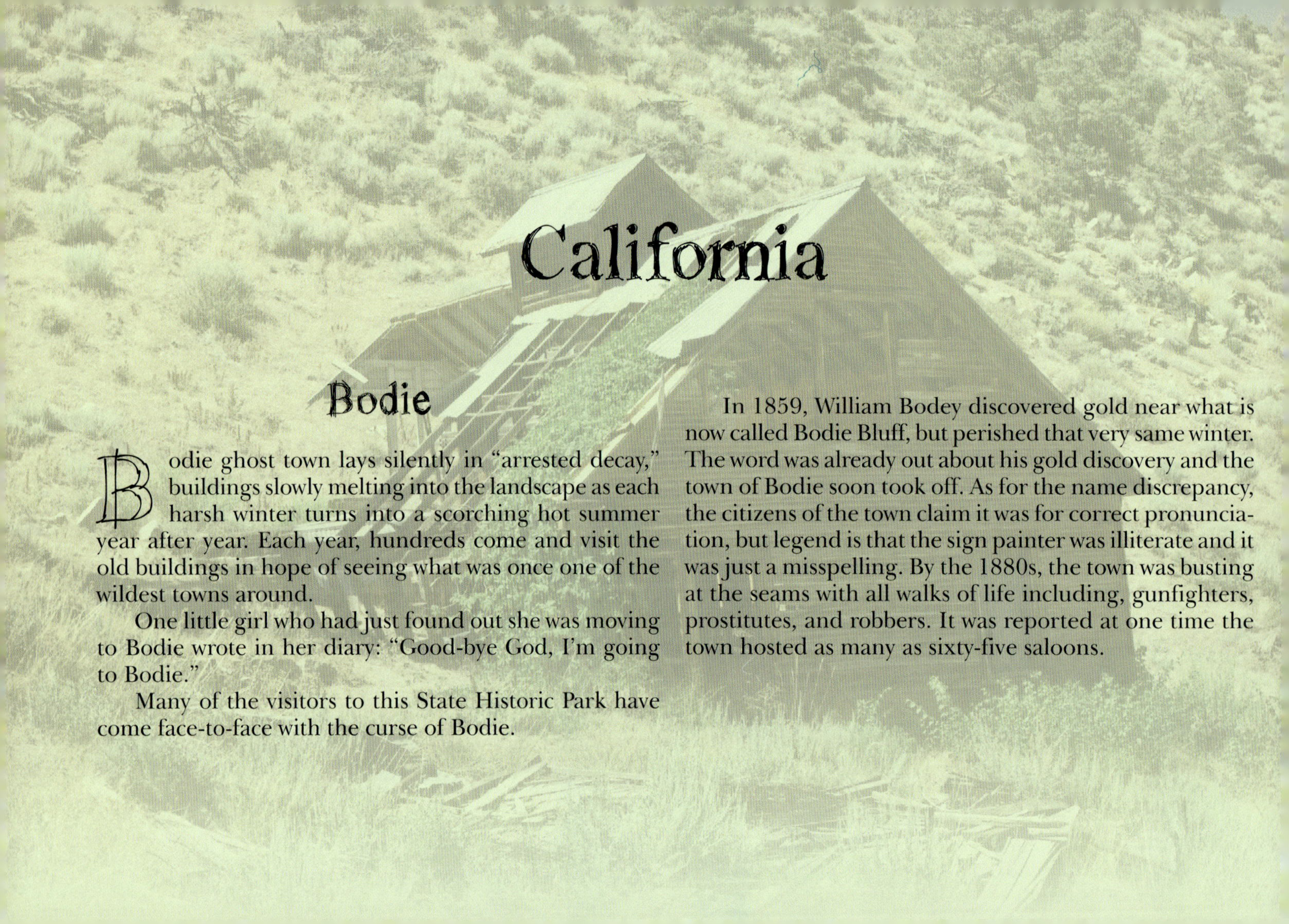

California

Bodie

Bodie ghost town lays silently in "arrested decay," buildings slowly melting into the landscape as each harsh winter turns into a scorching hot summer year after year. Each year, hundreds come and visit the old buildings in hope of seeing what was once one of the wildest towns around.

One little girl who had just found out she was moving to Bodie wrote in her diary: "Good-bye God, I'm going to Bodie."

Many of the visitors to this State Historic Park have come face-to-face with the curse of Bodie.

In 1859, William Bodey discovered gold near what is now called Bodie Bluff, but perished that very same winter. The word was already out about his gold discovery and the town of Bodie soon took off. As for the name discrepancy, the citizens of the town claim it was for correct pronunciation, but legend is that the sign painter was illiterate and it was just a misspelling. By the 1880s, the town was busting at the seams with all walks of life including, gunfighters, prostitutes, and robbers. It was reported at one time the town hosted as many as sixty-five saloons.

Don't tempt the Bodie curse when visiting this old town.
Courtesy of R.W.O'Brien

Courtesy of R.W. O'Brien

Courtesy of R.W. O'Brien

Courtesy of R.W. O'Brien

The undertaker never had a slow day in Bodie; between the miners blowing off steam in the bars and the card sharks that came to town to win, cheat, or steal some of the rich gold that was so prevalent, it was no wonder so many violent deaths occurred. The town's Methodist minister, Reverend F.M. Warrington, commented that the town of Bodie was a "sea of sin, lashed by the tempests of lust and passion."

The town slowly dwindled over time, and after two fires, not much remained. Two-year-old "Bodie Bill" was playing with matches one day and was responsible for destroying all but five percent of the town in 1932, leaving Bodie much as you see it today. After World War II, only six people were left in Bodie. Ed was one of those and in a drunken rage shot his wife. A three-man posse beat Ed to death for his crime. Soon after his death, the three men claimed to have been tormented by Ed, appearing to the men and shaking his fist in anger. The three men died within weeks of each other from strange diseases, the last resident in town soon left.

Some of the visitors to Bodie feel the need to take a piece of the State Park home with them but doing so brings on the Curse of Bodie. Even if a small rock is taken from the park, you will be cursed with bad luck. Some may think this is a bit of hogwash, but it is the truth according to the Park Rangers who have collected heaps of items including rocks that have been returned to the park by victims of this phenomenon. The long-deceased residents of Bodie are to blame for guarding the town against pilferers. In the museum, you can thumb through pages of letters that accompanied the returned items detailing the misfortune that followed the item home with the visitor.

The Cain House

Bodie has 168 remaining buildings, and yes, many of them are haunted. Park Rangers who have lived in the buildings have had many experiences. The Cain House has more than a few stories associated with it.

Jim Cain made a fortune bringing lumber to the desert town. All the houses in the town were made of wood. The scarce commodity was also needed for heat and the mills needed large quantities for their steam engines. Cain was wealthy enough to have a Chinese maid. It was not long before the rumors started that the two of them were having an affair. Horrified and embarrassed, Cain's wife promptly fired the maid.

A ghostly woman has been known to sit on residents of the Cain House.
Courtesy of R.W. O'Brien

Disgraced and unable to find work, the former maid committed suicide. It turns out in death she is not so fond of adults but loves children. One woman staying at the Cain house was startled one night to find a heavyset woman sitting on her while she was sleeping. The feeling of being suffocated choked the woman; she struggled to break free of the spirit. Finally after quite a fight she fell to the floor, free of her mysterious attacker. Another woman who stayed at the house reported hearing a woman's voice, and would sometimes hear music from the upstairs rooms when no one was there. The children of the house report seeing the ghostly face of the maid in their room; often the door opened and closed on its own as if she was checking on them.

Mendocini House

Another house the Park Rangers stay in is the Mendocini House. Children are heard laughing and playing around the outside of the house. A ranger who was staying in the house reported he heard what sounded like a party. Assuming the noise was coming from outside, he went to investigate, but the sound was vague. Upon returning, the noise from the party was even louder. He thanked the spirits for throwing him a party and asked them to stop and the house became quiet once more. Other common reports from the house are the smell of food cooking. When the rangers open the house back up after a long winter, they sometimes smell the fragrant aroma of an Italian meal cooking. Lasagna anyone?

Angel of Bodie

Evelyn or the "Angel of Bodie," as she has come to be called, is a three-year-old girl who was accidently hit in the head with a pick axe. The poor little girl was much loved as you can see from her headstone, a white marble angel. Evelyn has been seen laughing and merrily skipping along in the cemetery grounds. One visitor to the cemetery noticed his little girl playing with someone, someone he couldn't see; she claimed it was a little girl who lived there now. Evelyn has been heard in other areas of Bodie as well, out front of the Miners hall, a small girl's voice calling for her daddy has been heard by visitors on many occasion.

Eleanora Dumont

Eleanora Dumont came to Bodie near the end of her life. Dumont who later was known as Madam Mustache, once owned a beautiful gambling and prostitution house in Nevada City, California. Men were drawn to her establishment after hearing of her great card playing and the beautiful women she employed. Dumont had many suitors and was proposed to quite often but as with most tragic tales, she refused them all turning her attention to a handsome unattainable man. Editor Wait was the only man she wanted, he held the respectability that she could not obtain being a madam and cardsharp. Wait was not interested in a woman with such a social standing and married another.

Dumont was heartbroken and moved on to another town trying to forget about her only love. Over the years she accumulated several fortunes and lost them by the time she found herself in Bodie. By this time she was not as great a card player as she once was and turned to prostitution herself to survive. She had set up a blackjack table in one of the saloons in town and curious men came to play the notorious gambler; she always greeted them with a smile night after night as these men left her penniless. One night, after losing a hand of blackjack, she drank a shot of whiskey and staggered down the main street out of sight. The next morning her lifeless body was found a mile out of town in the fetal position. A small bottle of poison lay next to her, she was fifty years old, and had nothing left to live for. Among the personal items found on her was a letter requesting her body be buried next to her one true love in Nevada City, Editor Wait. The citizens of Bodie wanted to honor her wishes but the town could not raise enough money to send her to Nevada City and buried her in the Bodie Cemetery.

Visitors to Bodie have seen a shadowy figure walking along the road to Bodie, dressed in 1900s costume and crying silently. If she is approached, she vanishes. Others have also claimed to have seen her in the cemetery wandering among the graves seemingly looking for something. Is she looking for Waits grave? It appears that Madam Mustache cannot find peace until she finally is laid to rest next to her beloved in eternity.

One of the stranger spirits in Bodie is the mule who was killed in a mining accident. Visitors and rangers claim to hear the clicks from the mule walking nearby, and some claim to have even seen the animal. I could go on and on about the ghosts of Bodie, the lady who is seen peeking through an upstairs window, the children who haunt the schoolhouse, but alas I must move on and leave an element of surprise to the traveler who takes a step back in time.

The "Angel of Bodie" has been seen in the Bodie cemetery.
Courtesy of R.W. O'Brien

Calico

Nestled against the Calico Mountains, Calico ghost town is just that, full of ghosts. It all started in 1875 when prospectors first found a small amount of silver ore. In 1881, the town took off with prospectors flocking in to see if they could find their fortune. During its heyday, Calico hosted at least two dozen saloons, gambling halls, a public school, a church, businesses and a literary society. When the silver market dropped out in the late 1890s, so did most of the residents of the town. With so many people moving on, the town became deserted. In 1950, Walter Knott (the creator and former owner of Knotts Berry Farm in Buena Park, California) bought the old mining town with plans of restoring it. Knott spent much time visiting the town as a child where his uncle lived. The town as you see it now has both new and restored buildings, but that doesn't seem to deter the ghosts hanging around.

The Schoolhouse

The school seems to be a hotbed of supernatural activity. There is the little girl leaning out the school window waving to passersby, and another child who grabs visitors' legs and pinches their ankles, as well as a red floating light inside the schoolhouse. It seems the last teacher at the school is still around. One fantastic story that is often retold is about two British tourists. They thought they were speaking with a docent in period costume, but after returning home, they found out whom they were really speaking with, the ghost of Margaret Oliver. It seems the tourists took a photo with the woman and only after the photos were developed did they notice that the schoolteacher was mysteriously absent. After some inquiring, they found no staff member was working at the schoolhouse during their visit.

Does the owner still haunt this hotel in Calico? *Courtesy of J. O'Brien*

Glowing balls of light are seen floating in the Calico Schoolhouse.
Courtesy of J. O'Brien

The Boardwalk

Calico's main street boardwalk is full of spirits as well. The last marshal of the town, Tumbleweed Harris, has been seen. Walking along, or leaning up against a wall, he appears large in stature with a white beard. On Saturday nights, a long forgotten party still rages on at the Calico Corral. At Lil's Saloon the rumble of an old time piano is heard as well as clamorous crowds. Many of the employees of Calico have heard the jingling of spurs up and down the main street. The schoolhouse is not the only place you can see strange lights, clouds of glowing energy have been seen throughout town.

Postal Dog

Even a dog has been seen in town. The apparition of a Border Collie, Dorsey, the mail carrying dog, has been known to wander the streets or just lay in the shade seeking refuge from the hot desert sun. Dorsey was found laying on the postmaster's front porch, weak with starvation in 1883. He soon became a valuable member of the postal service carrying mail and messages to and from the nearby Bismarck Mine.

The Lane House

The Lane house is now the city's museum. It is the longest occupied structure in Calico. Lucy grew up in the town just above Calico. When she was eighteen years old, she married Calico native John Lane and they opened a general store in town. When the silver market dropped out in 1899, the couple left town like so many others but returned in 1916. They moved into their old store and then to the courthouse building. In 1934, John passed away but Lucy stayed on in the old town until her own death in 1967. Lucy must have really loved the little town, she still hangs around, many times sitting in her rocking chair taking in the sights. Lucy is recognized wearing a black lace dress walking between the store and her home. Clerks at her old store also hear unexplained noises and catch movement out of the corner of their eyes.

Hank's Hotel

The Hank's Hotel former owner is still around making sure visitors are behaving. One man, who was standing on the hotel's stonewall, was punched in the leg. Hank is known to tug on visitors' wrists and clothing, or is it another spirit of a young boy who hangs out in front of the hotel.

Calico
www.calicotown.com

Death Valley

Devils Racetrack

Death Valley is just that, it is the driest, lowest, hottest location in North America. With that in mind, there is a lot to Death Valley that is unexplained. One such place is known as Devils Racetrack or the Racetrack Playa.

A nearly level dry lakebed, the large boulders mysteriously travel across this plane. No one has seen these boulders move but they leave large ruts behind and can be tracked. One will move and another just next to it will not. They do not always move in straight lines some crisscross each other, some move in a curvy line. Several will travel a hundred feet then stop and turn back, as if they decided that way was the wrong way. They do not roll but rather slide across the dry desert bed.

Several theories surround these haunted rocks. The most popular theory is the wind moves them. Scientists have done experiments and they were able to determine it would take a wind speed of 580 miles per hour to move a 700-pound boulder. That couldn't happen, so what is making these rocks move?

Does something paranormal move these rocks? *Courtesy of BigStockPhoto*

Another idea is a thin sheet of ice forms on the basin floor, then if the wind picked up perhaps the rocks would move. This is not possible either.

Two men, Robert Sharp and Dwight Carey, did a study of the rocks in the late 1960s for seven years. They named the rocks and concentrated on about thirty of them. One rock, named Hortense moved 820 feet in one winter. Karen did not move at all but suddenly disappeared near the end of their study. Karen reappeared in 1996. Where did she go for so many years?

Since these rocks have never been seen moving, no one knows for sure what is going on. Are there spirits moving these rocks? Do they have a mind of their own? Are they looking for more suitable living climate? So many unanswered questions, but then again Death Valley didn't get its name for being friendly. One thing is for sure, I would not recommend camping out next to one of these rocks.

Amargosa Hotel and Opera House

If Death Valley wasn't creepy enough just to drive through, you can actually find quite a few places to stay the night. One such place is the Amargosa Hotel. In 1923, The Pacific Coast Borax Company built up a small town for the miners who were brought in to do borax mining. The town consisted of dorms, a general store, a hotel, a hospital, and corporate offices, as well as a recreation hall that provided entertainment for the workers. Today, much of the town is gone and is now known as Death Valley Junction.

In 1967, Martha Becket, a dancer from New York, was touring the area when her car experienced a blowout. Stopping to change the tire, Martha wandered around while her husband worked on the car. She stopped and looked through the recreation hall windows and immediately saw her future. She recounts the building spoke to her and she knew if she took care of it, it would take care of her.

Believing in fate, she knew she must stay. Remembering what a fortune teller told her before she left on the trip, she would move to a far-away rural area and the letter A would play a big role in it. While asking around about the building, she found out the town was called Amargosa before the Borax Company expanded it and took it over. The following day the couple leased the building.

Through the years Martha continued to perform in the recreation hall. With such a small population and a lack of tourists, she filled the walls with a painted audience. The painting did not stop with the auditorium, she continued throughout the hotel, some were portraits of people and other scenes, whatever struck her fancy at the time. Martha is still alive and kicking up her heels, usually just Saturday nights now, the audience is still limited, sometimes just the paintings watch her, and sometimes it's just the spirits that come to watch her.

Martha's former manager and husband still come to her shows, deceased now for many years, he is sometimes seen sitting in the theater or just standing on the sidelines making sure all goes as planned, cheering on his beloved.

The area of the hotel that hasn't been restored is called "Spooky Hollow," and for good reason. The area housed the original men and women's dormitories. Room 32 has a malevolent presence living in it. Records indicate a man was hanged in the room. It was also where the former manager resided while working for the mining company. A common complaint from guests is the baby crying in room 24, but after guests learn they are the only living occupant of the hotel, they usually are only too happy to leave quickly. Footsteps are heard in the hallways at night and lilacs are smelled all throughout the hotel. Trust me, nothing grows in Death Valley and lilacs would be very uncommon. Guests have reported having their shower turn on by itself, children giggling in the hallways and having their doorknobs turned and rattled only to find out no one else is in the hotel, not even staff. Room 9 is where the spirit relaxes in your bed not seeming to mind that you're sleeping in it.

The Amargosa Hotel and Opera House is listed on the National Register of Historic Places as well as the National Register of Haunted Places. Criss Angel even held a séance at the hotel in 2006 for one of his shows.

Amargosa Hotel and Opera House
Death Valley Junction, CA 92328
(760) 852-4441
www.amargosa-opera-house.com

Skidoo

The town of Skidoo sprung up after two miners lost in a thick fog found a bit of gold after setting up camp. The original name of the town was 23 Skidoo, the miners discovered gold on the twenty-third of January and the town featured twenty-three mining claims. Unfortunately, the United States Postal Service did not like the number twenty-three and shortened the name to just Skidoo.

In 1908, just one year after the town sprung up the local bartender shot the town banker for a mere twenty dollars. It was not long before an angry lynch mob took Joe Simpson into custody. A hasty gallows was built in the town center and Simpson was strung up for the shooting.

A reporter for the *Los Angeles Times* arrived in town to photograph the event; there was only one problem—Simpson had already been buried. The citizens of the town did not see this as a problem.

They quickly dug the decomposing body out of the ground, and reenacted the hanging with Simpson's lifeless body. The town's doctor saw this second hanging as an opportunity to cut off Simpson's head and test it for syphilis, a possible cause for his madness.

The spirit of an angry bartender roams the hills near Skidoo.
Courtesy of Library of Congress HAER CA-290-7

Simpson, twice hanged and headless now wanders the hills and valleys near where the sad remains of Skidoo now lingers. Treasure hunters to the area have seen his headless soul trudging along in the desert heat. Simpson's ghost seems to be looking for something. Justice? Or his head?

Tommy Knockers

The Cornish miners that came to the southwest to make their fortune brought some little helpers with them. Tommy Knockers are little gnome like miners, much like leprechauns or what the English call Brownies. The Cornish miners believed these little men were the souls of the Jews who crucified Christ and were sent by the Romans to work in the tin mines.

Often seen as green in appearance and wearing the clothes of miners they are both good and bad, when they are good they are really good and when they are bad they are very, very mischievous. The miners often would lose shovels, picks, or even the miners' meal; Tommy Knockers no doubt took them. Occasionally the Tommy Knockers would pick one miner to pester, blowing out his lantern, taking his tools, pelting the unlucky miner with stones just, of course, for the fun of it.

These little miners work side by side with men, picking away, looking for ore. Not many miners have seen them but they know they are there. Tommy Knockers have a good side too, they knock on the walls of the mine to warn of cave-ins.

Many of the Cornish miners would not work in mines until the mining company made sure the little miners were on duty. The mine owners put up with this nonsense because the Cornish miners were the best miners in the world, mining tin for centuries, they were highly skilled. The Tommy Knockers would work at one mine, never leaving until they were relieved of their duties. In 1956, one of the largest and oldest California mines was lobbied to release the Tommy Knockers from employment so they could be free to work the other mines in the area. The mining company agreed.

Colorado

Durango

The Denver and Rio Grande Railroad built a track from Silverton, Colorado, to the smelters in the mountains above Durango. Needing a place for the employees to live and trains to be maintained, Durango was established in 1880. The trains carried over three hundred million dollars in precious metals from the prosperous mines of Silverton to the smelters above Durango. The railroad is still there but no longer takes ore to the smelters; today, passengers are the only cargo riding the train from Durango to Silverton.

There are many ghost stories in this town, many of the buildings have a spirit or two, several of the spirits have inhabited the streets and some of them even ride the train.

Strater Hotel

Built in 1887, the Strater Hotel was pharmacist Henry Strater's vision. He overcame many obstacles to produce the dream of making it rich in Durango. He knew he wanted to build a grand hotel but he did not have the funds or the experience and he was a minor at the time. After much persistence and a little help, he finally realized his dream. Over the years, many writers stayed at the hotel. It was well furnished, quiet, but yet in the hub of things. Perfect for the artist who needed a place to write or something to write about, Mark Twain spent some time at the hotel as well as Louis L'Amore who wrote the Sackett Series at the Strater.

Henry Strater included a pharmacy in a corner of the hotel. Even though Strater built the hotel he did not want to run it, he wanted to focus on his pharmacy business, and leased the hotel to H.L. Rice. Rice kept the hotel upscale for a while until all the gamblers and prostitutes were forced out of Silverton and converged on Durango. Seeing this opportunity, he opened a gambling hall in the basement and spared a few rooms for prostitution. Strater was outraged but could not do anything since he had leased the building out. Strater was further infuriated when Rice raised the rent on the pharmacy to an outrageous price. Strater was inexperienced but wanted Rice out and came up with a plan. Strater built the Columbian Hotel just south of the Strater with the intent of putting Rice out of business. Over the years, both hotels stayed in business and prospered until 1895 when the silver panic put both of the men out of business.

Many hotels have journals the guests can write in; the Strater is one such hotel. In the Strater, many of the guests recount their terrifying unexplained experiences. Although the desk clerks deny the hotel has ghosts, with a wink of course, and rumors the staff has been instructed to tear out any ghost stories from the journal, you can still find a few entries they missed. I came across accounts from a journal in room 405 saying it is the most haunted room in the hotel. With such a hush over the ghost stories, who really knows which is the most haunted room. Next door in room 406 stories of bathroom toiletries flying about the room and hearing a gunfight in the hallway accompanied by the smell of fresh gunpowder and smoke riddle the journal.

On occasion, maids of the hotel find guests wandering into vacant rooms. When they follow the visitors in to assist them, the maids find no one. Freshly made bed linens are sometimes messed up when the maids just turn their backs for a moment, and several maids have been tapped on their shoulders when they are alone in a room. Voices are heard from rooms that are empty and tobacco smoke waifs through hallways; the hotel is now non-smoking only. It is common for guests to check out suddenly in the middle of the night due to all of the disturbances; some guests have even complained of seeing apparitions in the hallways—mainly a little girl who runs down the corridors, and mysterious knocking on their doors late at night. Other guests who have suddenly fled stated the water in their rooms turns on by itself and their clothes have been thrown around the room by an unseen force.

The Diamond Belle, the hotel's bar, has been a hotspot for another little ghostly girl who likes to play pranks on customers and tugs on their clothing. She has also been seen in the theater as well as a gentleman in Victorian dress. He likes to walk up on the stage then just disappears.

Strater Hotel
699 Main Avenue
Durango, CO 81301
(970) 247-4431
www.strater.com

Guests have fled in the middle of the night at the Strater Hotel in Durango.
Courtesy of BigStockPhoto

Railroad Stories

Since the railroad built the town of Durango, it's no wonder that so many ghosts are still around to keep the trains running smoothly. Many of the workers for the railroad have spirited tales to tell after work. One man claims to have seen a past worker wearing overalls floating around the roundhouse. He said the man floats because he has no legs after losing them in a railroad accident. Children's voices and footsteps are heard in the rail cars running up and down the aisles, laughing wildly.

One terrifying night a train stopped near Carbon Junction to switch cars, as the train started to move out of the area, a switch lantern came out of the nearby bushes. No one could be seen carrying the lantern. The engineer watched as the lantern floated to the train, up the stairs, and then to the top of the train, then back down to the other side and off the train again and disappeared.

Right:
Train roundhouse in Durango where dead workers still tend to the engines.
Courtesy of Library of Congress, LC-USF34-037716-D

Mesa Verde

Built in the sixth to the twelfth century, the Indian dwelling built into a canyon wall is now deserted, only frequented by the many visitors who come wondering why the Indians just walked away from their homes. The Anasazi Indians have come to mean "ancient people" although in the Navajo language it means "enemy ancestors." The name came about after the discovery of the ruins in 1888 by Richard Wetherill a rancher and trader. The descendants of the Anasazi prefer the name Pueblo Indians and many of them still live in the region today.

Apparitions of the Anasazi Indians are seen walking around the Cliff Palace, they are mainly seen near the kivas at the base of the canyon. The kivas are subterranean rooms used for religious rituals. Each kiva has a pit in the floor that was used as a portal to the spirit world. Maybe the Anasazi are using the portals between the spirit world and ours. The Balcony House is another place where the ancient Indians are also seen roaming around their old homes.

Right:
Visitors to Mesa Verde have seen the spirits of the ancient Anasazi walking around there old home.
Courtesy of Library of Congress, LC-USZ62-101891

Clift Pal
N° 7

Ancient Anasazi still walk among the visitors at Mesa Verde. *Courtesy of R.W. O'Brien*

Anasazi Ruins *Courtesy of R.W. O'Brien*

St. Elmo

The Starks

Several children were playing in St. Elmo's Hotel when all of the sudden the temperature dropped and all of the doors slammed shut at the same time. The children ran out as quick as their little feet could carry them and never stepped foot in the hotel again.

The ghost town of St. Elmo in Colorado was settled in 1878 when men came to the area looking for gold and silver. The town had hopes of being a nice family town but with all the single men in town, unsavory businesses soon appeared, saloons, gaming halls, and brothels were soon filling the streets.

In 1881, Anton Stark moved to St. Elmo. His wife, Anna, ran a general store and the Home Comfort Hotel. The couple's three children worked at the store and hotel and as their wealth grew so did their status in the town, but Anna was said to be humorless and stern with the children. The children rarely left town and were not allowed to socialize with any of the town's children.

Mines started closing in 1910 and the population dwindled until finally, in 1922, all but a few residents were left, just the Stark family. The railroad tracks were torn up and the town was officially finished. However, the Starks still kept hope the town would come back. They quickly started buying up the properties in town until they owned them all. After a few unsuccessful attempts to bring mining back, they turned to tourism, but that failed, too. The general store stayed in operation until Anton Stark died. Their daughter convinced Anna it would be best if she moved to a nearby town for work, reluctantly Anna agreed. Annabelle soon met a man and they got engaged but the marriage never came to be, and devastated Annabelle moved back to St. Elmo. Her mother and older brother both died in 1934; Annabelle and her brother Tony were the only two residents left in St. Elmo.

The siblings lived at the hotel with no running water or electricity, they never changed their clothing for weeks or months and they took to hoarding everything they could find. To make the matter worse, Annabelle started patrolling the town at night, brandishing a pistol to anyone she saw. People started calling her Dirty Annie and most thought she was crazy. Finally, it was too much and friends had the last of the Starks committed to a mental institution. The pair straightened up in the institution and were released after just a few weeks. Her brother died soon after and Annabelle found new residence at a nursing home where she died. St. Elmo was left to a friend.

The friend who inherited the town decided to restore the hotel; she hired her grandchildren to help clean out the piles of rubbish that filled the hotel's rooms. It seemed that no matter where the children left things, the next day the items would be piled in the middle of the room. Everyday this happened without fail. The woman kept up the cleaning and just took the mysterious happenings as Anna trying to help. Many visitors to the town also have seen a young woman in early twentieth-century clothing in the second-story window looking out. Many of the locals believe this is Annabelle's ghost trapped in the hotel forever.

In 2002, a fire swept through town and destroyed six buildings including the Starks original residence. A few people still reside in St. Elmo, but they live side by side with the spirits of the miners, gunslingers, and store owners who died in that town.

Trinidad

The Tarabino House

www.tarabinoinn.com

The Tarabino House was built in 1907 by two brothers who were so close they built a single family home for their two families. The Tarabino Brothers started the Famous Department Store in downtown Trinidad, and were also involved in real estate and ranching in the area. The home the brothers built for their families was constructed in a U-shaped Italianate style with a carriage house in the back; each brother had a wing for their families. The two brothers eventually moved to California where they died years apart but at least one member of the Tarabino family owned the house until it was sold in the 1960s. Today it is a bed and breakfast.

Several spirits enjoy the bed and breakfast, one a young lady, manifests in a nightgown at the top of the stairs. She appears to be interested in the guests and owners of the house. Another spirit the owners call Hector emits a strong cherry cigar smell in the library. Smoking is no longer allowed in the house and the smell can be quite overpowering at times. Several reports of a loud crash have been reported, vibrating the whole house. On one occasion, plaster from the ceiling came tumbling down. When the noise is investigated nothing can be found out of place. On another occasion, a guest to the house reported seeing someone sitting on the foot of her bed. She thought it was her husband, but then noticed him lying next to her fast asleep. When she looked back, the apparition had disappeared. A previous owner to the property states she encountered two young children on the stairs at night; frightened, she screamed and they disappeared as quickly as they came.

A sensitive stayed at the house and claimed the ghostly children haunt the second story. Two different women walk up and down the staircase, a man (Hector) is in the library, and Barney Tarabino himself is at the residence. Barney has been seen sitting on the front porch in a top hat and suit and one guest said Barney paid her a visit in her room the previous night, actually tickling her while she lay in bed.

An unearthly presence is felt in one bedroom, though nothing bad has happened, it is still unnerving. Visitors often feel a presence in the house, as if someone or something is watching them and some have even refused to enter certain rooms or areas of the house.

A wave of energy is said to flow through the house. Two different "experts" have claimed this and one even says he can see it from the street.

Nevada

Carson City

Mark Twain

President Lincoln appointed Mark Twain's older brother Orion Clemens to a secretary position in the new territory of Nevada in 1861. Orion built a home in Carson City and sent for his wife, Mollie, and his daughter, Jennie. In 1864, at the age of nine, Jennie contracted meningitis and died with her most loved uncle by her bedside.

Mark Twain was very close to his niece, he often stayed at his brothers house while working in nearby Virginia City. Jennie was buried in the Lone Mountain Cemetery in Carson City. Mark Twain was so disgusted with the undertakers that handled Jennie that he wrote the story "The Undertakers" and began a lifelong battle against the overcharging of undertakers' services. After her death, Mark Twain's writing became more sarcastic and hard-hitting.

Jennie Clemens is still seen roaming the graves near where she is laid to rest.

Courtesy of R.W. O'Brien

rtesy of R.W. O'Brien

Courtesy of R.W. O'Brien

Over the years since Twain's death in 1910, many people claim to have seen Twain by his beloved niece's gravesite as well as in his brother's home in Carson City. Jennie is also said to be still hanging around. Jennie has been seen in the Lone Mountain Cemetery, she appears to be translucent, in a white dress strolling along the headstones, perhaps waiting for her uncle.

Genoa

Sam Brown's Goin' Down

Sam Brown came to the Carson Valley in the 1860s, he was a mean coward who would only lay prey to those who were unarmed or off guard. Brown had one mission in life, to be the chief of all bad men in the Comstock. By 1860, he had already murdered a handful of men along California's coastal towns and had done a stint in San Quentin, finally landing in Virginia City. Upon arriving, Brown stabbed a helpless drunk to death and soon after he jabbed his bowie knife into the heart of another man who had mistakenly bumped into Brown at a saloon. In the following year, Brown took the lives of four more men bringing his death count to twelve in the Comstock area. It was not long before everyone in the area feared the outlaw.

On Sam Brown's thirtieth birthday, he declared he should have a man for supper. Brown made his way down the mountain from Virginia City heading towards Genoa. Along the way he picked up a riding partner, Alexander Henderson, one of a few men willing to ride with the killer. Brown stopped at Webster's Hotel between Carson City and Genoa, where Brown though Mr. Webster would be a good target. Webster was ready to defend himself and charged after Brown. Brown quickly retreated and headed to Genoa. Robert Lockridge was at the Genoa Bar, it was clear to Brown that Lockridge was not going to go down easy and decided to continue on, without fighting Lockridge. Brown and his trail partner kept moving on until they came across Van Sickle's Station.

Van Sickle was a quiet and respected man in the Comstock. Van Sickle came to the Comstock from New Jersey; along the way he had been an Indian fighter, bullwhacker, and blacksmith. Finally settling south of Genoa, the Van Sickle Station was a stop on the emigrant trail and a place for the Pony Express riders to switch to fresh horses.

The gun that was taken from Sam Brown's dead body as a souvenir.
Courtesy of R.W. O'Brien

Van Sickle and his friend Wheeler were talking on the porch of the station as Brown and his partner rode near. Van Sickle called out to the riders thinking they were the Pony Express riders come to change mounts. Brown yelled back at Van Sickle that he was here to kill him and pulled out a revolver shooting towards Van Sickle. Van Sickle then ran inside where dinner was being served. As Brown chased the man in, the dinner crowd stood up blocking the sight and a path between the men. Brown quickly ran out seeing that he was overpowered.

Many of the dinner guests consoled their host, among much talk it was decided that Van Sickle should go after Brown instead of living in fear that he would come back and kill him unannounced. Van Sickle had no other choice than to pursue Brown until he was dead. Grabbing his double barrel shotgun Van Sickle jumped on his horse and took chase, not even taking time to clear out the birdshot, which was left in his gun. Soon Van Sickle was close enough to take a shot and hollered to Henderson to get out of the way, which he did quickly. Van Sickle fired both barrels and shot Brown's hat off. Van Sickle quickly reloaded with the shells he brought with him and Brown jumped off his horse and took refuge in a nearby house.

Several riders from Van Sickle Station were now in pursuit with plenty of ammunition. Henderson met the group and bragged he had shot Brown claiming that Brown had been bragging all day he would have a man for dinner. Brown exited the rear of the house and kept on riding trying to escape Van Sickle who was now determined to kill Brown rather than live in fear of his own life. Brown now approached Israel Mott's house where he again hid from Van Sickle. Approaching, Van Sickle called out and to Levi Miles who had come out of the house when Brown entered. Levi announced that Brown had gone out back. Now dark, Van Sickle dismounted and crept along until he heard Brown's Spanish spurs and fired both barrels, hitting Brown directly in the chest. Van Sickle's dinner guests had now arrived after following the sound of gunshot. Several of the men shot into Brown's lifeless body, celebrating that the most feared man in the area was now dead.

Men came from as far as San Francisco to thank Van Sickle for killing the notorious Sam Brown and Van Sickle was later rewarded by being elected the first sheriff of Douglas County. Brown's body was temporarily stored in Lute Olds' barn across the road from where Van Sickle shot him.

The Lute Olds' barn is the same barn where the prospector by the name of Sawtooth was thrown under some potato sacks after being murdered for his satchel of gold. Sawtooth was the only man to have found the legendary Snowshoe Thompson's lost mine. Men are still looking for the lost mine today.

Is this the barn where Sawtooth and Sam Brown still hurl potatoes?
Courtesy of R.W. O'Brien

Local residents to the area recount that soon after Brown's death, the two men, Sawtooth and Brown, were seen at the barn heaving potatoes and shaking the rafters nightly. One man, Fritz Dressler, claims the two men are still raising hell in the barn. Dressler recounts how he was thrown across the barn by the spirits and pelted with phantom potatoes. W.F. Skyhawk wrote a poem about the ghostly events at the barn (1943 *Pony Express Courier*):

> Down came robbers from the canyon!
> Down from the Border Ruffian Range!
> Stealthy slinkers in the darkness!
> Hear the story weird and strange:
> Came the horse thief gang one evening
> As the clock struck midnight hour;
> Blazed their guns that killed old Sawtooth
> Close beside his water tower.
> Looted they and silent laid him
> Shrouded 'neath potato sacks.
> Thence came Sam Brown's ghost to join him,
> And they run but leave no tracks.
> Phantoms romp, and nightly frolic,
> Till Old Sol proclaims the dawn,
> Spirits shake the eerie rafters
> Sockety-eyed, and faces wan.
> Ghosts of Sam Brown, and of Sawtooth,
> In that haunted cellar rule.
> Venture not lest you inflame them!
> Be not kindred to a fool!
> Fairview's barn is gruesome haunted,
> And forever is its doom.
> Where the ghost heave big potatoes
> One heaved Dressler' cross the room.

Gold Hill

Gold Hill Hotel

Just down the hill from Virginia City is the small town of Gold Hill. It sprang up around the Yellow Jacket Mine. One of the buildings which has not crumbled through time is the Gold Hill Hotel.

The Gold Hill Hotel started out as the Riesen House, according to the state archives, and was most likely built in 1861 (owners state it was 1859) by Miss Louise Forster and Alfred Riesen. The two partners ended up selling the hotel but leased it back as the Gold Hill Hotel. The winter of 1861-62 was an unusually wet one and shortly after the hotel's completion, it sustained damage from the floods, which resulted from the snowmelt. The southwest and southeast corners of the building fell, leaving the main part of the building. By the end of 1862, Forster and Riesen ended their lease and moved on.

The next owner of the hotel was Horace Vesey and his son, Edward. They renamed the hotel the Vesey House. Vesey House was quite popular and held such events as the Vesey Ball, an upscale cotillion party. Vesey moved on in 1867 and managed a few hotels in Virginia City. By 1907, the building was a private residence and the town had all but died with the economic decline. Buying the building in 1958, Dorothy and Fred Inmoor renovated and added an addition to the structure.

The Gold Hill Hotel today has nineteen rooms and several other houses or structures you can rent for the night. The main hotel also holds a restaurant and a main great room where you can come to one of their many events including storytelling and Dinner Theaters.

The hotel has many ghosts that reside in its walls. Rosie is the woman who hangs around room 4; she is often smelled more than seen with a fragrant aroma of rose water that follows her around. Rosie has been known to shake keys, jewelry, and even the change in your pocket. Room 5 is William's room; he is thought to be a criminal who was shot when he was caught cheating in a card game or, as some speculate, a miner who may have perished in the Yellow Jacket Mine disaster. Many visitors smell his cigar smoke; many describe it as a cherry blend. Room 11 is where the children's spirits like to play, they pull the covers, tickle your feet while you are sleeping, and lock the bathroom door on you. I mentioned the rooms that are most associated with the particular spirits but they are seen and play all over the hotel and you may experience Rosie on the stairs or hear William's heavy boots walk into the bar.

The spirits Rosie and William keep guests and staff on their toes at the Gold Hill Hotel. *Courtesy of R.W. O'Brien*

The Miners Lodge can be rented for the night as well. This building was used as a washroom and bunkhouse for the Yellow Jacket Mine. The morning of April 7, 1869 was a disastrous one. A fire broke out killing thirty-four men. Many of the bodies of these men could not be recovered, and the fire raged for many years after in the mine shafts. This was not the only disaster in the Yellow Jacket Mine; daily there were deaths from mining accidents, ranging from severed limbs to explosions and cave-ins.

Some of the men who died at the mine still go about their daily lives and come up to the Miners Lodge to rest. Guests to the cabin report whispers late at night from the miner's spirits and sometimes even conversations being heard from unknown areas of the building. Cameras and other battery-operated equipment seem to fail without warning. One guest of the lodge experienced a spirit sitting and lying down on his bed as he tried to sleep. He claimed it happened repeatedly throughout his stay there.

Gold Hill Hotel
1540 North Main Street
Virginia City, NV 89440
(775) 847-0111
www.goldhillhotel.net

Lynch House

Just three houses down from the Gold Hill Hotel, the Lynch House is now a beautifully restored rental house for vacationers. Instead of tearing down and replacing items with replicas or new, the current owners took the time and had the original pieces of the house repaired and put back in their original place, including the fence outside the house.

The house was built by Simon and Marie Ogg in 1869. The house was very decadent for its owners; it included several parlors, three fireplaces, and four bedrooms. The couple soon opened a livery stable next door. Besides housing your horse, the livery stable advertised carriages, buggies, and rockaways for rent.

As the mining industry came and went the Oggs fell upon hard times and lost their house in 1881, this was not the first time they'd lost their house to foreclosure, but it was the last time they would buy it back. Twenty years later, in 1901, Simon would die of paralysis at the age of sixty-two.

The Oggs had lots of drama in their lives; besides living beyond their means, they also lived through any parent's nightmare when their seven-year-old daughter was raped at a neighbor's house. Charles Pohl, who was the caretaker of the house their daughter was visiting, was accused of the deed. Newspaper reports of the time recount how the man forcefully took the innocence of Birdie Ogg in the home of Mr. Fox. This was not the worst of it. Pohl was diseased and left little Birdie diseased as well. Birdie did not initially tell what had been done, but when she came up lame and could hardly walk, she confessed to her parents what had happened at the home of Mr. Fox.

Initially, Pohl was ordered out of town, but this decision was recanted after the arresting officer, being a father himself, decided that was not enough punishment. Now there was a diseased child in his town which brought shame to the family. Pohl was held on $5,000 bond and went to trial for the rape.

The house changed hands several times from 1881, and finally, in 1903, was bought by the Lynches. In 1906, another tragedy happened to a Lynch. Martian Lynch's wife, Margaret, suffered a great loss when her father was literally blown to pieces in a mining accident at the nearby Buckeye Mine. Her father, Daniel Carroll, was thawing a box of powder on a forge at the blacksmith's shop. The box exploded and his body was blown apart. The trunk of his body was found sixty feet away. The fragments of his head, legs, and arms were found over several acres. If that was not enough, Daniel's heart and liver were found at the bottom of a chute for dumping mine ore. Margaret's father was known to be five-ten or -eleven feet tall; his parts were buried in a box smaller than four feet.

When the current owners started renovating the house, a strong smell of cigar smoke was present. The house's previous owner smoked cigars but it was quite a different smell that now permeated the rooms—an old-fashioned cigar blend. Could it be a past owner of the house checking in on the renovations? Even now, guests claim to smell the strong aroma of cigars, even though smoking is not allowed on the property. The present owner and guests to the Lynch House have also felt a presence of a young girl following them around, could that be little Birdie who was raped in a nearby home. Footsteps are heard walking around the rooms when no one is present as well as breezes that come seemingly from nowhere. The current owner just wants to co-exist with the spirits, hoping they are pleased with the renovations she has made to update the house as well as the restoration to preserve the past. Sorry, as I finished up this book I received word that the Lynch House is no longer a rental house.

Goldfield

Goldfield Hotel

In 1902, the boom town of Goldfield sprang up. Many notable men came to the mining town including Virgil and Wyatt Earp to open saloons, banks, restaurants, and hotels. One such hotel was the Goldfield Hotel.

Built in 1908, just a few years before the town went bust, the Goldfield Hotel was the finest around, offering guests 154 decadent rooms, telephones, electricity, crystal chandeliers, and gold leaf on the ceilings. It was considered one of the most luxurious hotels west of the Mississippi River.

Shortly after the hotel was built, it was sold to George Wingfield, the owner of Goldfield Consolidated Mines. Unlike a lot of the rumors about the hotel, George never lived there. His partner, Casey McDannell, lived at the hotel and managed the property.

In 1923, the hotel sold again to Newton Crumley whose plan was to mine under the hotel for gold. His two mine shafts revealed only dirt and rock, no gold was ever found. By the 1930s, Goldfield, which once held more than 35,000 people, barely supported a population of 1,000. The hotel became a flophouse. When World War II broke out, the hotel became home to the Army Air Corp personnel stationed at the Tonopah Air Base, twenty-five miles away. The hotel was vacant by 1945.

The once grand Goldfield Hotel then went through numerous owners over the decades, each promising a great revival, all have failed in their attempts for restoration. By 2003 the hotel had fallen into ill repair, the county auctioned the property off once again hoping for a new owner to bring the hotel back to its former state. One bidder put in an offer on the hotel for $360,000 dollars. A rancher from Carson City named Edgar Roberts is now trying his hand at restoring the hotel. Roberts is planning on renovating the bottom two floors into forty rooms for rent as well as a casino and café.

Many people have speculated why no one has been able to restore the Goldfield Hotel; there are those who assume it's the ghosts who want the building left as it is, decaying back to the earth. One such ghost still resides at the hotel. Elizabeth is said to have been a prostitute George Wingfield kept company with. After she became pregnant, he chained her to the radiator until the baby was born, disposed of the baby down a mine shaft under the hotel and then starved Elizabeth to death. Now, if you paid attention, earlier I said that George never stayed at the hotel, and the mine shafts were dug out much later than when George owned the hotel. I do not want to speculate who Elizabeth was, but in room 109 a woman's spirit resides. She is wearing a white flowing dress and has long hair. Workers at the hotel in the past have refused to work in that room for fear of Elizabeth. Down by the mine shafts a baby is heard crying; is that Elizabeth's baby?

Elizabeth may be the most famous but by far not the only spirit at the hotel. The colorful cast of ghosts includes children who are seen playing and are heard giggling in the hallways, even the spirit of a little person who likes to poke and tap unsuspecting visitors at the hotel. There is the "Stabber" in the Gold Room (the main dining hall). He wields a large kitchen knife at anyone who crosses into that room. He has never actually hurt anyone but frightens them as he appears suddenly and then disappears as quickly as he came. Two people committed suicide in the hotel. One is a woman who hung herself and the other is a man who jumped to his death from the window of his third-floor room. The two of them are seen wandering the halls of the third floor, unable to find peace. Cigar smoke is smelled and fresh ashes litter one of the first floor rooms. Many psychics have toured the hotel, many of them claiming the hotel is one of the seven portals to another realm.

As I write this story the hotel is still only occupied by its many spirits with no signs of opening anytime soon.

Ruby Mountains

Armbruster Pike

While the Donner Party was trying unsuccessfully to cross the Sierras into California, Armbruster Pike was leading another group to California, but this group was a few weeks behind and crossing the Ruby Mountains in northern Nevada. The same storm that stranded the Donner Party stranded the Pike Party. While waiting out the storm, the Pike Party also ran out of supplies and started looking for an alternative food source. No one knows if Armbruster was murdered and then eaten or died from starvation and the elements, but when the group was finally able to move on Armbruster was not with them.

The surviving members of the group reached their destination of California, but not without the guilt of

Ready to Write a Book!

We're always seeking authors for a wide variety of topics. This is your opportunity to shine! See our website to view an extensive list of our titles. If this idea appeals to you, we'd love to hear from you. Review our book submission guidelines at our website by clicking on the "Submit a Book Proposal" link. Then email your proposal and ideas to **info@schifferbooks.com** or write to the attention of **Acquisitions** at the address below. You can also call 610-593-1777 to make an appointment to speak with an editor.

Schiffer Publishing
has books covering a wide
variety of interests including:

Antiques, Collectibles, & The Arts

Advertising • Automobilia • Black Collectibles • Breweriana • Ceramics • Clocks • Corkscrews • Decoys • Dolls • Fine Art • Folk Art • Furniture • Graphic Art • Holidays • Hunting • Jewelry • Kitchen • Lighting • Leatherwork • Metalware • Native American Crafts • Nautical • Pinball • Quilts • Rugs • Sports • Teddy Bears • Telephones • Textiles • Toys • Video Games • Vintage Fashion • Watches • Writing Instruments and more.

Design, Lifestyle, & D-I-Y

Architecture • Astrology • Counter Culture • Culinary Arts • Erotica • Interior Design • Kitchens and Baths • Landscaping • Numerology • Paranormal • Pin-Ups • Pop Art • Tarot • Tattooing • Textile Design • UFOs • Witchcraft • Basketry • Beads & Jewelry Making • Carving • Furniture Making • Gourds • Home & Garden • Metalwork • Modeling • Pyrography • Sculpture • Textiles • Weaving • Wood Turning • Tools and more.

Military, Aviation, & Automotive History

WWI & WWII Armor/Aviation: German • U.S. • British • Russian • the Jet Age • Unit Biographies and Autobiographies • Edged Weapons • Firearms • Uniforms and more.

Maritime

Seamanship • Navigation • Ship Management • Towing • Transportation • Boats & Boat Building • Medical • Legal and more.

Regional

History • Children's Books • Architecture • Photography • Landscaping • Paranormal • Souvenir • Guidebooks • Cooking and more.

To learn more, go to **www.schifferbooks.com**
Call 610-593-1777, 8:30a.m.-5:30 p.m. EST
or write to 4880 Lower Valley Road
Atglen, PA 19310 USA
and ask for a free catalog(s).

In the UK and Europe contact
Bushwood Books at 44 (0) 20 8392-8585
info@bushwoodbooks.co.uk

Bookmark printed in China

what had happened. Luckily, it was overshadowed by the Donner Party's tragedy and not much was heard about them as life went on. Armbruster Pike seemed to still be around though, not in the flesh but in spirit. Ever since that winter of 1846, people have claimed to see him in the desert, with his long white hair and beard.

One rancher had an encounter with Armbruster he will never forget. While out looking for some lost cattle, the rancher came upon a man leaning over behind a bush. As he came closer to see what the grizzly old man was doing; he saw the man eating the carcass of a cow with his hands. Blood from the cow covered the old man including his beard and the ends of his long white hair. Even more frightening, the rancher claimed the old man had no legs, just a torso floating above the ground. The rancher seeing this horrific sight left as quickly as he could, not wanting to end up like the dead cow.

Lots of mines exist out by the Ruby Mountains, and just like the rancher many of the miners have had encounters with Armbruster. In the 1980s, many of the men who worked on the night shift had unexplained events happen to them. Equipment would start up on its own including haul trucks. Some of the drills used would stop working without any reason only to start up again when the equipment or Armbruster felt like it. Some of the miners even saw the figure of Armbruster walking along, all alone, always hunched over with white hair and beard and invisible legs.

One night in January, a man was out camping with his two dogs near the Ruby Mountains when all of a sudden the dogs started growling.

The legless ghost of Armbruster Pike wanders the roads in the Ruby Mountains. *Courtesy of R.W. O'Brien*

Their hair went up on their backs and they seemed quite disturbed. All during the night they would make a twenty-five foot loop around the campsite, but would always return just as bothered. In the morning, the camper walked about to see if he could find any animal tracks or any sign of what may have been bothering the two dogs. Nothing was in the snow except for the two dog tracks. Was it Armbruster looking for food?

If you're in the area of the Ruby Mountains, make sure to look out for Armbruster Pike. He may just be looking for some fresh meat...or a new pair of legs.

Courtesy of R.W. O'Brien

Virginia City

In 1859, Peter O'Reilly and Patrick McLaughlin were in six-mile canyon looking for gold when the miners came upon strange looking black dirt, uncommon, since most of the soil was a yellowish gravel. After putting the black soil in their rocker they were astonished by the pounds of gold left behind. Henry Comstock soon heard about the great find and convinced the two prospectors their claim was on his land. This claim became the richest on the Comstock Lode. Henry Comstock cashed in his stake in the Ophir Mine for a mere ten dollars and opened a store in Carson City. After losing his business, he wandered through Idaho and Montana prospecting. On September 27, 1870, Comstock shot himself near Bozeman, Montana.

Hearing of the gold strike, a flock of miners rushed into the six-mile canyon soon after Virginia City sprung up. The biggest problem the miners had was the blue-gray mud that stuck to their picks and shovels. When the mud had been assayed, it proved to be filled with silver ore.

Virginia City soon became the most important settlement between Denver and San Francisco. Instantly prospectors became millionaires, building mansions and importing the finest furnishings from Europe and Asia.

The new wealth of the small mining town brought on a population boom along with many notable residents and visitors such as Samuel Clemens. Clemens came to Virginia City in 1862 and worked for Nevada's first newspaper the *Territorial Enterprise* earning just twenty-five dollars a week. By the time Clemens left Virginia City a mere twenty-two months later he was known as Mark Twain.

George Hearst also got his start in Virginia City. In 1860, Hearst purchased one-sixth share of the Ophir Mine for $3,000, and received a profit of $91,000, enough to take over ownership of the Homestake Gold Mine and Anaconda Copper Mine.

Over the years, Virginia City has developed a reputation as one of the most haunted cities around, no doubt because of all the deaths that occurred since the 1880s.

Julia Bulette

All but a few fortunate cribs are gone now on D Street. One that did not survive through the years was Julia Bulette's small house. Julia was an honorary member of Virginia City's fire department and well liked by the majority of residents in the mining town.

Many stories about Julia portray her as some sort of angel helping to take care of the sick and the elderly, beloved by all, could do no wrong. She was loved by many but in reality she was just a prostitute struggling to survive like most of the working girls at that time. Julia did not work out of a sporting house. She rented a one room house called a crib on North D Street and had a few regulars who enjoyed her company.

Julia's life was snuffed out the morning of January 20th, 1867, and she walked into history. The previous night, Julia's company was enjoyed by a miner, the following morning a Chinaman entered her home as he did every morning to build a fire. He noticed Julia was still sleeping and was careful not to wake her. About eleven o'clock that morning her neighbor came by to call her for breakfast and discovered Julia's lifeless body. The coroner's report stated she had been beaten with a piece of firewood, smothered with her pillow and then finally strangled, the thumbprints still visible on her throat. Some of Julia's belongings had been taken making this brutal crime appear to be a robbery.

Julia Bulette was murdered in a crib much like this one.

Julia's body was then taken to Mr. Kitzmeyer, the undertaker, who had been enamored with her. He quickly filled her coffin with sand and buried Julia in his basement to keep her close to him forever. Julia's coffin was buried on Flowery Hill, as she was not a respectable woman and could not be buried in the cemetery proper. Her grave is now lost but her spirit remains in the old funeral parlor on C Street and the area where her house stood on D Street. The funeral parlor has long been closed to the public but tales of objects moving are common, including stories from residents and visitors to the building of Julia's spirit appearing suddenly, then vanishing. Is Julia really buried in the basement of the old building? No one knows for sure, maybe it's just a wild rumor that has traveled through the ages. Some visitors to Virginia City have claimed to see a transparent likeness of her wandering Flowery Hill as well.

Katie Hillyer

Katie Hillyer, a writer local to Virginia City has been seen on Virginia City's main street after her death in 1968. One of her favorite things was to visit the bookmobile that used to visit the town. Many local residents have seen her wearing her favorite old jacket and baseball cap that was always planted on her head. Not only has she been seen on the street but also in some of the bars that line the main drag, C Street. Reports from one bar state she was seen leaning on the railing smiling and nodding as if silently saying hello, but seems quite detached from the real world.

Ophir Mine

In January 1859, Henry Comstock discovered the now famous Comstock Lode in the Ophir Mine site. Comstock befell bad fortune when developers swooped up the mine from under him. The residents of Virginia City ran to the Ophir Mine on a night in 1874, thinking a fire had broken out by the bright beam of light, which shot out of the opening of the mine. No smoke or flame could be found, just the strange light that rose from the shaft. The next morning strange unexplained occurrences started happening at the mine, noises were heard emitting from the shaft, a cage was summoned when no one was in the mine. When the men went into the mine, they found the spirit of Henry Comstock claiming he had returned to reclaim his gold. Reports from the onlookers say he had chunks of flesh hanging from his decomposing skeleton. Comstock remained at the mine and continued to play tricks on the miners, blowing out the candles, summoning the cage, taking the men's tools and placing them in different areas of the mine. The miners who continued in spite of the harassment often were terrified by the horrific laughter that echoed through the mine shafts. Today the mine is closed; ol' Henry Comstock must be happy, finally having his mine to himself once again.

Silver Queen Hotel

The Silver Queen Hotel is said to be one of the most haunted buildings in Virginia City. Reports from guests, visitors, and employees of the hotel include a combustible fight echoing throughout the halls and ending with the sound of a man chasing a woman through the halls. A white mist has also been seen floating through the hotel including some of the guest rooms. Knocking on the guest room doors are often heard late at night, with no one at the door. There are also reports of a young girl walking around in the hotel. One guest at the hotel claimed to have heard a banjo in the room next to him, later to find out no one was staying in the next room. Another guest checked in, dropped off her luggage, and went out on the town; when returning she found her bed was all ruffled up like someone had come in and rolled around on the bed. Several other guests I spoke to claimed to mysteriously have found a pink or red feather on the floor after waking up in the morning, perhaps it was Rosie's, one of the resident ghosts.

Is the Silver Queen Hotel where two spirits still have a long forgotten fight? *Courtesy of R.W. O'Brien*

The hotel is kept in its nineteenth-century state; the only modern amenity is the electricity and the running water. There are no televisions, no radios, no internet, phones, or other electronics. Is the hotel kept in this state because when you do bring in electronics, none of them work? Cell phones do not get reception in the rooms and if you leave them on the bureau, batteries are always dead by the morning. Cameras tend to go through batteries rather quickly as well in the hotel.

Silver Queen Hotel
28 North C Street
Virginia City, NV 89440
(775) 847-0440

The Washoe Club

The Washoe Club was once a getaway for the millionaires of the Comstock. The building was one of the lucky ones to have escaped the great fire of 1875 with the fire only entering the building and not engulfing it. You can still see the charred bricks in the back room behind the pool tables. The building also holds one of only two non-supported spiral staircases, the other, Loretto Staircase, is in Santa Fe, New Mexico. Behind the bar is the original mirror that was shipped from Europe and brought over the mountains in the 1860s.

In the back of the first floor is where the spirits of today are kept cold in the natural cellar, but in the 1800s the area was used to store the bodies from mining accidents, murders, and the many other perils of the time. In the winter months, when the ground was frozen in the Silver Terrace Cemetery, the corpses were kept in the cellar until the spring thaw, sometimes piling up as high as B Street on the hill behind the building.

The Millionaires Club moved to the second and third floors of the Washoe Club after the great fire when the building which housed them burned down. Secret staircases riddled the building allowing the members of the club to go about any sort of business they wanted in private, including prostitutes, who frequented the club, secret meetings among the city's elite, and not to forget gambling.

With all the activity that went on in the building, it's no wonder the club is haunted. If you stop by for a drink, you may want to take a close look at the man next to you. A ghostly miner smelling of ether is said to appear at the bar and commandeer drinks from unsuspecting patrons.

"Lena," as the locals like to call her, appears all over the building, but especially on the spiral staircase. She appears in a haze, feet floating just inches from the floor dressed in early Victorian clothing. "Lena" is also known as the lady in blue. She was murdered in the 1870s by one of her clients. Some say her throat was slit in an upstairs bathtub; others claim she got into a fight with the manager and was pushed down the spiral staircase.

Washoe Club's staircase, a spirit of a woman has been seen peering down from it.
Courtesy of R.W. O'Brien

Through the second story windows you may be lucky enough to see another of the unlucky prostitutes; she appears in a negligee pacing back and forth in front of the windows.

One common accident in mining towns was people getting run over and hurt by horses, carriages, and wagons. Such a tragedy happened outside the Washoe Club when a young girl was run over by a carriage. She was hurried into the Club and unfortunately expired in the bar. Her spirit has been seen and heard on the spiral staircase and upstairs on the second floor crying for her mother.

It's not just the miner that likes to interact with the customers and employees of the Washoe Club, women who use the restroom might have the surprise of being locked in, only for the door to open suddenly as if nothing had happened. Other visitors to the club who have been lucky enough to have visited the second and third floors, which are now closed to the public, have reported having their rears pinched and slapped by an unseen hand.

There are so many spirits in the Washoe Club, I could fill a whole book on them, I will leave you with these few tales and hope when you visit you may experience one for yourself.

Washoe Club
112 C Street
Virginia City, NV 89440

MacKay Mansion

In 1859, George Hearst built the MacKay Mansion as a Gould and Curry Mine office and home for the mining superintendent. Hearst only kept the house briefly and moved on after making a few million dollars from the Comstock.

In the early 1870s, John MacKay acquired the three-story brick home and with his partner, James Fair, parlayed a few unsuccessful claims into the Consolidated Virginia Mine. The partners then discovered the largest silver deposit of the time in the North American continent. The mine produced a total of one hundred thirty-three million four hundred seventeen thousand dollars in silver.

MacKay was uncomfortable with his new found wealth and spent most of his time and money helping the unfortunate. MacKay died in 1902 en route to London for a business transaction, he was seventy years old.

The MacKay Mansion is now open to the public as a museum. You can walk the halls and see where MacKay and his partner, James Fair, slept, ate and spent their spare time, as well as the mining office that started it all. The mansion does not allow overnight guests except for once when Johnny Depp stayed at the mansion while filming the movie *Dead Man.*

John MacKay's house where Johnny Depp saw a spirit of a little girl.
Courtesy of R.W. O'Brien

Johnny Depp has been quoted saying he believes in ghosts and one of the reasons he wanted to stay at the MacKay Mansion was because of the many spirits that reside there. Depp was not disappointed; he claims to have seen a spirit of a little girl in an upstairs bedroom. The bedroom across from where he stayed is the nursery, set up with a child's bed and lots of toys. It's no wonder that a little girl would hang out there. Depp also claimed to have heard a child's laughter and giggles coming from the nursery.

Another spirit at the MacKay Mansion is that of a former Army Colonel who often appears to be sitting at the kitchen table. A former servant is also thought to be the one hurrying up and down the stairs and makes different unexplained noises on the third floor while she tidies up the house. The last ghost that is said to stay at the house is a woman who is seen sitting in the parlor in a high-back chair. She is thought to be the lady of the house and is heard upstairs on the third floor possibly checking on the servants work.

MacKay Mansion
129 South D Street
Virginia City, NV 89440

Mark Twain Museum

The Mark Twain Museum is located in the basement of the old Territorial Enterprise building. It houses many of Twain's personal items including his writing desk. There are several reports of Mark Twain hanging around his favorite haunts, including his desk in the museum.

The building is one of the oldest in town, surviving the great fire of 1875. Built in 1862, it has held a bank, hardware store, auto shop, and gas station. Twain was in his twenties and just honing his writing skills when he lived in Virginia City. Being that he was still young and not married, he used to hang out a lot with the other writers in town, many times frequenting the different bars of the area. One of his favorite places was Pipers Opera House as well as the Washoe Club.

Mark Twain Museum
23 South C Street
Virginia City, NV 89440

Is Mark Twain still writing from beyond the grave at his desk in Virginia City?

New Mexico

Albuquerque

La Placita Restaurant

Built in 1706 by the Armijo Family, the La Placita Restaurant was used as a residence for many years until the American Civil War. During the Civil War, the building was used as a fort and refuge for locals in the area who had lost their homes. After the war, the building was used as a trading post and finally abandoned. The years of hot summers and cold winters took its toll on the building, and in 1930, the building was in near ruins when it was restored to its present condition. A restaurant now occupies the structure along with several ghosts.

A total of four spirits haunt the quaint Mexican restaurant. Elizabeth who is seen in the restaurant and around the old town is the most common. She lived behind the restaurant and died of tuberculosis at about the age of eight—usually she is carrying her doll. Many of the patrons report seeing her in the bathroom mirror; the bathroom was her bedroom in the late 1800s. Another spirit calls out employees' names. No one has seen George, as they have come to call him, but he enjoys playing pranks on the staff. The other spirits are Victoria who is seen wearing a wedding dress and an angry woman who stays mainly upstairs. The spirits that reside at the La Placita Restaurant have been known to appear as glowing lights or cold spots. However they choose to manifest, they must feel at home in the restaurant since none of them seem to want to leave.

La Placita Restaurant
206 San Felipe Street NW
Albuquerque, NM 87104
(505) 247-2204
www.laplacitadiningroom.com

The Böttger Mansion

A bed and breakfast now stands where the territorial Governor's residence once stood, it was a forty-room adobe mansion. In 1908, the mansion was torn down and The Böttger Mansion was built in its place.

Charles Böttger wanted the best of everything and the mansion had the first electric lighting in Albuquerque, speaking tubes (the equivalent of a modern-day intercom), a dumb waiter, a coal fire central heating system, and a basement, which was uncommon for the area. The mansion was dubbed the "Pride of Old Town." Böttger was also the first man in town to own an automobile.

As the years passed, the money started to run out and Böttger began to take in boarders to make ends meet. Many celebrities stayed at the mansion. Machine Gun Kelly even stayed for a time until suspicions grew high and Kelly, along with his gang, fled town. Elvis Presley and Janis Joplin also stayed at the Böttger, and Frank Sinatra performed in the courtyard for a wedding reception.

The money never came back for the Böttger family, though, and the house and land were eventually sold. The 1970s provided the mansion with a short revival housing an art gallery, beauty parlor, and miscellaneous other businesses. In 1989, the Böttger Bed and Breakfast opened and has been occupying the mansion ever since. Even when there are no paying guests, the rooms are always filled with spirits.

There is between three and six ghosts that reside at the mansion. Charles Böttger pops up a lot; he has been known to pace the parlor and stairway, and has walked into guests' rooms, opening doors and checking on guests as they sleep.

Another spirit likes to mess with the well-earned sleep of guests and is known as the "lover." This spirit usually lies down in bed with pretty young women; when the guest turns over to see who it is, no one is there.

The "grandmother" spirit just sighs a lot in disapproval. She is Böttger's grandmother who in her old age was locked outside one chilly night causing her to catch pneumonia. Rumors spread that her grandchildren were trying to speed up her death for the inheritance.

A weeping woman has been seen in a room that used to be the wine cellar. She usually appears as a smoky form crouched in the corner with her hands cupping her face, weeping inconsolably.

Other spirits who may be causing some of the activity in the house include an American Indian woman who tripped on the stairs and fell to her death. Doors open and close, lights turn on and off, and on one particularly hot day, a window in the mansion that was painted shut opened by itself to let in the cool air. Dishes have flown off shelves and a toilet downstairs has been known to have its lid opened and closed. Objects placed on top of the toilet have flown across the room.

The Böttger Mansion Bed and Breakfast
110 San Felipe
NW Albuquerque, NM 87104
(505) 243-3639
www.böttger.com

Maria Teresa's Restaurant

Built in 1783 by Salvador Armijo, this twelve-room hacienda in the center of Albuquerque has at its heart an enclosed patio. The home has changed hands several times throughout the years and now is the Maria Teresa's Restaurant—and the most haunted building in New Mexico.

According to reports there are at least four different spirits at the restaurant, a few have even been known to dine with unsuspecting customers. One customer glanced up at a mirror while he was enjoying his dinner only to notice a man in a dark suit sitting next to him. When he looked directly at the chair, the man he'd seen was not there.

Another spirit who likes to make herself known is an older woman with black hair streaked with gray wearing a long beaded dress. She is seen rearranging silverware and checking on the patrons.

Still another older woman dressed in red is believed to be Armijo's daughter. The apparition smells of perfume and appears in the doorway leading to the dining room. Guests have described her as having dark hair and light eyes.

An apparition of a woman in her early thirties has been seen in the Zamora Room. She is referred to as a woman of refinement and poise, with long flowing dark hair, wearing a white dress.

The bar is where the cowboy is seen, dressed in chaps and vest. Always standing in the doorway, he has only been seen from one particular table in the bar area of the restaurant.

Besides the apparitions that are repeatedly seen, unearthly voices are heard throughout the building, plates and glasses and even tables have moved on their own, and employees have quit on the spot after encountering a whole room of spirits.

Maria Teresa's Restaurant
614 Rio Grande NW
Albuquerque, NM 87104
(505) 242.3900

Alcalde

The Old Alcalde Courthouse

As the story goes a young señorita from Spain came to Alcalde to marry her betrothed. Her father who arranged the marriage was very proud of this match and only wanted the best for his only daughter. The match was made with a Frenchman who was very wealthy and could provide quite a comfortable life for the senorita. Soon after they were married, they moved into a large Hacienda and started their life together.

Not long after, she caught the eye of a man in town with her beauty. This drove her jealous husband mad with rage. During one argument, he forcefully hit his wife; she lost her balance and fell down the stairs breaking her neck. Despondent over killing his wife, he too threw himself down the stairs where he was found lying next to his lovely wife.

Several years later, the home was turned into a courthouse, the men who were found guilty of their crimes were hung from the tree in front. The employees of the courthouse often reported seeing a young beautiful woman in period costume walking around the second story and on the staircase. Her husband, the Frenchman, has been seen pacing one of the second-floor offices which was renovated from a bedroom. Out front on the old tree still hangs the spirits of the convicted, swaying in the breeze.

Today the building is vacant, abandoned by everyone except the spirits, passersby have seen lights in the building even though the electricity was turned off long ago.

Cimarron

Lambert Inn/St. James Hotel

Henry Lambert built the Lambert Inn in 1872 in Cimarron. Henry was originally from France and came to America to serve as the personal chef to President Abraham Lincoln and General Ulysses S. Grant, but left service to search for his fortune in gold. Lambert finally settled in nearby Elizabethtown, but found that mining was not his forte.

The Lambert Inn soon held a bloody past, with more than twenty-six killings in the building. Many of the locals would ask over morning coffee who was killed the night before at the Lambert. It was a rough saloon and restaurant with a few rooms for rent, but by the 1880s, it had grown into a full-blown hotel offering forty-three rooms. In 1901, the roof was replaced and roughly 400 bullet holes were revealed.

Everyone who was anyone stayed at the hotel, including, Wyatt and Morgan Earp and their wives, who stayed at the hotel for three nights on their way to Tombstone, Arizona. Jessie James always stayed in room 14—notorious in his own time, he signed the register as R.H. Howard. Jessie James' cousin and killer, Bob Ford, also stayed in the hotel. Buffalo Bill Cody met with Annie Oakley at the hotel and talked to her about his Wild West Show. When he left town to hit the road with his show he took most of the area's Indian population with him. Other celebrities of the time who stayed at the hotel were Black Jack Ketchum, Kit Carson, writer Zane Grey, General Sheridan, Billy the Kid, Doc Holliday, Bat Masterson, the Governor Lew Wallace, Pat Garret, Fredrick Remington, and Clay Allison, to name a few.

The town of Cimarron soon would dwindle in population as the gold ran dry. The Lambert Inn quickly fell into disrepair. The inn changed names through the years and finally came to be called St. James Hotel. In 1985, the hotel was restored to its former glory as a luxurious hotel and is now open to the public. You too can stay at the hotel and sleep in room 14 where Jessie James slept and see the twenty-two bullet holes in the restaurant's ceiling.

The St. James Hotel has nearly enough spirits to fill the hotel to its capacity. Room 18 has been kept vacant for the spirit of James Wright who won the hotel in a poker game. He was not lucky enough to become the owner, though. Wright was killed as he returned to his room, shot from behind as he opened the door; he chooses to stay at the hotel even after his death. (Wright does not like company with him in his room.)

A former owner of the hotel said she was pushed down while cleaning Wright's room, and on another occasion saw a brilliant orange ball of light hovering in the corner. Before the room was closed off to the public, a number of the guests who stayed there were mysteriously found dead the next morning.

If you wondered what a ghost would need in a hotel room, the St. James has apparently fulfilled Wright's wishes after death and furnished his room with a bed frame, no mattress, a rocking chair, a basin and pitcher, and a coat rack for his ghostly clothes to hang. Some personal items left for Mr. Wright include a container of ACE Copenhagen, a bottle of Jack Daniels, a deck of cards, several shot glasses and a painting of a half-naked lady. Apparently, that is all a nineteenth-century ghost man needs in a room.

A ghost still has a room at the St. James Hotel.
Courtesy of Library of Congress, HABS NM, 4-CIM, 7-1

The next room is where Lambert's second wife mainly resides. Elizabeth is the hotel's protector. She gave birth to her children in the hotel and later died there in December 1926. Her favorite perfume, a rose scent, is often smelled in the room. Sometimes, when the window of the room is open, a tapping will be heard until the window is closed and even reports of a transparent woman fitting her description is seen in the room.

Another of the famous spirits of the hotel is that of a dwarf-like old man. He is reported to be quite mischievous, nicknamed the "little Imp" by the hotel staff. He likes to play tricks on the employees, hiding objects which are later found. Many times just his creepy laughter is heard echoing through the hotel and restaurant.

Other activity at the hotel includes smelling cigar and cigarette smoke, cold spots, electrical equipment failing or acting on its own accord. One former manager of the hotel saw a cowboy-like figure standing behind her in a mirror in the bar but when she turned around, no one was there. Lights are reported to turn on by themselves and doors spring open or slam shut.

St. James Hotel
617 South Collison Avenue
Cimarron, NM 87714
(575) 376-2664
www.exstjames.com

Cloudcroft

Cloudcroft Lodge

The woman, irritated by the continual ringing of the phone in her room, called down to the front desk. She exclaimed that all night long, the phone had been ringing and when she answered, no one was there. She would hang up, just to have it ring again. The man at the front desk apologized and explained Rebecca must have been calling her.

Rebecca came to The Cloudcroft Lodge in the 1930s seeking employment; the beautiful red head was hired immediately as a chambermaid. It was not long before she had several suitors, one of which was a burly lumberjack with a quick temper. One afternoon, he came off the mountain early and surprised Rebecca. She was in the arms of another man, and in a rage, he murdered the beautiful woman and quickly disposed of her body. Rebecca was never seen again; only later was her body discovered buried in the basement where the workers' quarters were.

Rebecca is now seen wearing a long flowing nightgown all over the hotel. She especially likes the Red Dog Saloon located in the basement. Ashtrays are known to slide across tables, lights turn on and off by an unseen hand, and the most unusual activity are the 1930s-era poker chips that suddenly appear in the middle of the floor. Guests to the hotel often complain of loud honky tonk music coming from the saloon, when the saloon isn't even open. On occasion, an apparition of a woman has been seen quietly dancing alone in the bar.

Guests and staff to the Lodge have seen Rebecca drifting quietly down the hallways or sometimes stopped at a table arranging one of the many floral arrangements, but one guest got a little extra one night. The gentleman came in late from a long day of sightseeing. He immediately went into the restroom to prepare for bed when he noticed a beautiful red headed woman taking a bath in his room. He rushed out and found an employee in the hallway a few doors down. Upon returning, the woman had vanished but wet footsteps had appeared on the carpet of his room and continued out his door into the hallway. He had not seen anyone leave his room and he was just a few doors down.

The Cloudcroft Lodge was built in 1899 by the Alamogordo and Sacramento Railroad. The log-constructed building was lavishly built and quickly became a favorite among Southwesterners wanting to escape the heat. The hotel offered a restaurant, billiards, tennis courts, golf, a dancing pavilion, burro trips, and a children's playground. In 1909, the Lodge was destroyed in a fire, but the embers barely cooled before the new hotel was built. This new hotel was just as grand as the previous one; in fact, it has quite a dossier. Clark Gable, Judy Garland, and Pancho Villa are among some celebrities who have stayed at the Lodge.

If you are lucky enough to stay or visit the Lodge, don't mind the phone calls. It's just Rebecca on the other end of the line.

Cloudcroft Lodge
601 Corona Place
Cloudcroft, NM 88317
(800) 395-6343
www.thelodgeresort.com

Cuchillo

Old Cuchillo Bar and Hotel

Old Cuchillo Bar and Hotel is located in the ghost town of Cuchillo, a mere thirty-five residents call the once-thriving town home now. A stagecoach stop, the bar offered weary travelers a place to pick up mail, supplies, a meal, and a room for the night.

Cuchillo was founded by ranchers and farmers around the 1850s. Named after the Apache Chief Cuchillo Negro, the town soon blossomed as it lay midway between the silver mines at Winston, Chloride and Hermosa. After the mines closed and the highway bypassed the town, residents soon left and the town started to deteriorate.

The Cuchillo Bar and Hotel once again will offer a few of its previous amenities, including cold beer and a room (presently only rooms are available). The building and town has plenty of former residents still hanging around, including one spirit that whistles old cowboy melodies and another that knocks glasses off the bar. The current owner has experienced lots of paranormal activity in the building. He has related that a voice whispers in his ear and that once he woke from a dead sleep to disembodied voices filling the air.

Do rats or spirits knock glasses off the shelf behind the bar in Cuchillo? *Courtesy of Josh Bond*

Courtesy of Josh Bond

Courtesy of Josh Bond

Courtesy of Josh Bond

Another eerie experience occurred in the bar when a group of people saw an old photograph hanging on the wall blink. At the same time, a loud bang roared out behind the group, but everything was in its place. What could have caused this noise, and how did the woman in the picture blink? The previous owner of the bar heard the old stove door open and wood being stacked inside; with no one around to do this chore it must have been a bit unnerving. Additionally, ghostly dark shadows are seen in the doorway and doorknobs rattle and turn.

Old Cuchillo Bar and Hotel
Hwy 52
Cuchillo, NM 87901
www.CuchilloBar.com

Other Cuchillo Haunts

In another house, the resident claims the former owner never left. A feeling of an older woman cooking is felt in the kitchen and of always being followed through each room. The owner claims it is a warm comforting feeling, but eerie nonetheless.

Residents who grew up in the town remember chasing after balls of light which are seen in the flats above Cuchillo. The residents would jump on their horses and chase after these mysterious lights, always out of reach, but it seemed the lights would roll along with the riders, teasing them further away from town until they finally would disappear. On other occasions, balls of lights would appear and seem to go beyond the flats, up hills, and finally blend in with the stars. Are these lights UFO's or the spirits of Apache Indians protecting their land?

Elizabethtown

A Mystery in Elizabethtown

Abandoned buildings now litter the ground that once housed more than seven thousand citizens of Elizabethtown. Just one year after the civil war, Captain William H. Moore found an injured Ute Indian and brought him back to Fort Union where he nursed him back to health. Ever thankful, the Indian gave Captain Moore some of the pretty rocks the Ute Indians used for trade. After closer inspection, Captain Moore recognized them as being rich with copper. After speaking with the Indian, he agreed to take the Captain and two of his soldiers to the upper slope of Baldy Mountain where the rocks were found. As the men set up camp later that night, a few took out their pans and began sifting the nearby creek, it was not long before gold was found. Immediately, the group forgot about the copper find and went on to search for gold. As winter quickly approached, the three men carved the words "Discovery Tree" on a fir next to their camp and headed back to Fort Union.

The news spread through the camp quickly and by the next spring, men poured into the area setting up camp to search for their riches. Captain Moore and a few other men formed the Copper Mining Company in 1867, soon after the first lode of gold was found. Quickly, Moore opened up a general store and started plotting the town. Captain Moore named the town Elizabethtown after his daughter who had just turned four years old. Elizabeth lived there all her life and became the first schoolteacher. Elizabethtown soon grew, and by 1869, had over 100 buildings, including saloons, a red light district, gambling halls, and more respectable businesses, like sawmills and churches. In 1870, with over 7,000 residents, the town was recognized as a rapid-growth area and the territorial legislature created a new county, Colfax County, with Elizabethtown as the new county seat.

Most new mining towns of the west had a diverse cast making up its population; Elizabethtown was no exception. Charles Kennedy, a large man with a wild beard lived in a cabin near Elizabethtown. It seems that Charles had more in mind for the travelers than a pleasant meal and place to rest for the night; around fourteen people went missing after staying the night with him.

It took quite a while for the men to show up missing, and in the fall of 1870, Kennedy's terrified wife came into town hysterical and fearing for her life. She found her way to John Pearson's saloon, where she told her story to a few of the local ranchers. She recounted how after luring a traveler to their cabin for a meal, Charles, the traveler, and their son sat down to eat. When the traveler asked if there were many Indians around, Charles' son exclaimed that the pungent smell that filled the cabin was not the food but was an Indian burning in the fire. In a rage, Charles stood up, and shot the traveler, then bashed his son's head into the rock that made up the fireplace. Then he locked his wife in the cellar and drank himself into a stupor. His wife waited until Charles had passed out, then climbed up the chimney and ran into town. A group of ranchers and the sheriff arrested Charles and searched his cabin. They found two skeletons in the cellar and many more charred body parts in the fireplace. Charles was held at the town's jail to await trial.

Meanwhile, Charlie's attorney boasted around town that he was sure Charles would get off and be set free. The local legend is that on October 7th, 1870, the quick-tempered gunslinger, Clay Allison, and his gang broke into the town's jail, tied a rope around Charles' neck, and dragged him behind his horse through town until he was dead. Then, the story gets a bit gruesome. Allison cut off the murderer's head and carried it to the nearby town of Cimarron where he insisted the head be displayed in front of the St. James Hotel, which was called the Lambert Inn at that time. (However, the Lambert Inn was not yet built. In fact, Henry Lambert, the owner of the Lambert Inn lived in Elizabethtown at the time of Allison's incident with Kennedy.)

By 1872, Elizabethtown's growth cooled as the mining operations diminished; New Mexico government noticed this and the town lost its county seat. The town did not die though; a baseball team was formed and traveled to nearby towns for games. People from all over the area came into Elizabethtown for popular dances which were held even in the middle of winter. At that time, a group of young men started coming to the dances and were welcomed for their good manners and snappy apparel. It was later found the young men were part of "Black Jack" Ketchum's gang. It appeared they spent their days robbing trains, stores, and banks, and their nights charming the locals. It was not until they were later captured that the townspeople found out their true identities.

Elizabethtown, the spirit of a serial killer still roams the streets. *Courtesy of Library of Congress, LC-USW3-019043-E*

The town barely hung on through the years with mines closing all the time; people moved out of town daily. The town finally died when in 1903 a fire broke out and engulfed most of the town. A few buildings still survive today; a museum is the only business in town, run by an Elizabethtown descendant who is slowly trying to restore the dilapidated town.

You can still see Charles Kennedy's wooden grave marker at the cemetery and sometimes even Charles roaming the countryside looking for weary travelers.

Granite Gap

Hidden Gold

Once home to two thousand miners and their families Granite Gap was mined for its silver, lead, zinc, and copper. The temporary town of tents and adobe buildings dwindled in population and the buildings melted back into the earth. Johnny Ringo passed through Granite Gap often, and in 1879, won two mining claims in the area from a card game. Nothing much is left at Granite Gap but the area has a lost treasure legend.

In 1882, the Curly Bill Brocius Gang of eight men robbed the Benson-Tombstone Stage and came away with eight gold bars, one for each man. After the robbery, all of the eight men scattered in different directions. Two of the men, Dutch John and Little Dave, rode together to Lordsberg stopping at Granite Gap to rest their horses. After setting up camp, Dutch John settled down for the night, and while he slept, Little Dave took an axe and struck Dutch John, decapitating him. Little Dave then took both bars of gold and buried them near the trail to Granite Gap. Little Dave set out for Oklahoma, and after settling down, he returned to Granite Gap to retrieve his booty. Unfortunately, spring floods washed out the trail and he could not identify where the gold was buried. Somewhere out there are two gold bars still waiting to be found, but be careful if you try your luck finding them. A disgruntled Dutch John without his head and Little Dave are also still looking for their gold bars.

Watch out if you're looking for lost gold in Granite Gap; two outlaw spirits are looking for it as well.
Courtesy of R.W. O'Brien

GRANITE GAP
GHOST TOWN

Treasure hunters who have camped out in Granite Gap have reported experiencing the sounds of wagons and horses coming through the valley. Near the old mining tunnels, swaying lights have been seen at dusk and dawn.

Lincoln

Billy the Kid

Lincoln, New Mexico will always be remembered thanks to several events that happened in the late 1880s with Billy the Kid. Two men, Lawrence Murphy and James Dolan owned the only store and bank in Lincoln County, which encompassed one fifth of the New Mexico territory. The pair also had several large cattle ranches and had many influential ties with the politicians in Santa Fe. Due to their large number of holdings in the territory, they had their hand in just about everything, including law enforcement and price fixing. The local farmers and cattlemen were not so happy with the monopoly the pair had on the economy of the area.

It wasn't long before another store popped up in town. Alexander McSween and John Tunstall soon started taking business away from Murphy and Dolan, which set off the Lincoln County War. Most of the fighting was done through cattle rustling and gunfights, finally escalating when John Tunstall was shot; then, as he lay on the ground, his skull was bashed in with the butt of his own gun.

Tunstall's men wanted revenge, one of which was none other than Billy the Kid. The "Regulators," as they called themselves, went on a killing spree, leaving a trail of bodies in their path of anyone who was involved with Tunstall's murder. The war came to a head in July of 1878; a fierce gun battle occupied the town. The Regulators took refuge in the Ellis Store and McSween's house. The fighting finally ended after the U.S. Army intervened. Five Regulators including McSween had died, and only one of the Murphy-Dolan group had perished. Even though the Murphy-Dolan group won, Billy the Kid became famous. Governor Wallace then stepped in and proclaimed amnesties for all who were involved in the Lincoln County War—all except for Billy the Kid.

Being a fugitive Billy took off and formed a gang; they survived mainly by rustling cattle. Billy's old friend, Pat Garrett, soon caught up with him and jailed him in the Lincoln County Courthouse. Billy was not one to wait around to die. Before he could be hanged, he somehow got hold of a gun, and while everyone was across the street at dinner, he shot his one jailer and waited for the sheriff, who he gravely disliked, to emerge from dinner. As Sheriff William Brady crossed the street, Billy unloaded a shotgun into him. Calmly, Billy then gathered up his belongings, borrowed a horse, and slowly rode out of town.

Lincoln County Courthouse where spirits are still on trial.
Courtesy of Library of Congress, HABS NM-216-1

Lincoln County Courthouse

Many of the original buildings that stood when Billy was there are still around today and still in use. The Lincoln County Courthouse still stands, now as a museum. Many people visit the courthouse each year and some return home with mysterious stories to tell. Some visitors tell of footsteps that follow them around, strange noises that emanate from empty rooms, and the sense of disapproval from a large crowd. Is it Billy that is still escaping from the room he was held in, the deputy and sheriff that Billy shot down, or the many others that faced justice in the building?

Lincoln County Courthouse
988 Calle La Placita
Lincoln, NM 88338
(575) 653-4372
www.nmmonuments.org

Ellis Store and Inn

The Ellis Store and Inn where Billy and his group stayed and sought refuge during the five-day battle of the Lincoln County War. It is another building that is still in business and taking guests, that is if you don't mind the resident spirits staying with you.

Jinny and David, the owners of the Ellis property, recant some of the most common occurrences that have happened to guests or to themselves. Guests on many occasions talk of their door opening and closing at night even though the lock is on the inside of the door; many just think it is the innkeepers checking on them. It is not until the morning they find out about the female spirit that is really checking on them.

On one occasion, a male guest told a story over breakfast that he woke from his sleep to a woman wearing a purple 1880s dress standing over him in bed. Other male guests have had the same experience of waking to see her standing by their bedside.

A ghostly presence of a woman has been seen at the Ellis Inn.
Courtesy of R.W. O'Brien

Jinny also tells of butter knives mysteriously moving; she would find the flatware later under flowerpots or on windowsills. The most frightening experience would be a woman's vociferous laughter suddenly echoing through the house. Jinny has experienced it all—lamps plugged in suddenly unplugged, doors and windows opening and closing, strange smells and noises she cannot explain away. A friend who painted a mural in one of the bathrooms returned a few days later with a painting of a woman whom he saw in the house. He said the woman wanted her picture to hang in the living room. The guests and owners have described the woman he saw as the resident ghost. Her picture will always hang proudly in the living room.

Ellis Store and Inn
US Route 380, Mile Marker 98
Lincoln, NM 88388
(800) 653-6460
www.ellisstore.com

Mesilla

Double Eagle Restaurant

Located in the central plaza of Mesilla is a regal one-story adobe house. Once the home to the Maes family, it has now become the Double Eagle Restaurant. The Maes family was a proud group, especially the mother who had the highest expectations for her eldest son, Armando.

Armando had other plans; he had fallen for one of the servant girls, Inez, and would do anything to be with her. His only obstacle was his overbearing mother; she had plans for him to marry another from the aristocracy in Mexico City.

As time went on, the couple's secret glances and walks in the town center aroused speculation and whispers among the servants and villagers. The Señora soon caught on, forbid the couple to see each other, and promptly fired Inez.

One afternoon the Señora returned home early from a trip to discover the young lovers in Armando's room. As she stepped back in shock at her sons disobedience, the Señora tripped over her sewing basket. In haste, she grabbed her shears and lunged at Inez, stabbing the beautiful woman in her chest. As she lunged for a second time, her son, horrified, leaned forward to shield his lover. Armando took this blow to his back. The servants hearing such a commotion rushed to the room just in time to see Armando kiss Inez one last time before she passed away. He then looked up upon her last breath to the upper corner of the room, as if watching someone. The Señora horrified at what she had done cried out for her son, but he refused to look at her.

Armando died three days later, never looking at his mother again. The Señora never uttered another word; her last word until her death years later was Armando, her son's name.

Today, the room called Carlotta Salon was formerly Armando's bedroom. Two large chairs newly re-upholstered adorn the salon. The cut velvet is worn where in each chair a person would sit. One worn mark is larger than the other but still small by today's standards. Perfume is smelled in the restaurant when no one is around, glasses which are set up the night before are found broken the next morning in the Carlotta Salon. After the alarms are set and the restaurant has been locked for the night, doors are found opened without setting off the alarm.

On one occasion a former employee set out two glasses of wine, he made a toast to the spirits and drank one glass, leaving the other on the table still filled with wine. When he returned to work the next morning the alarm had not been set off but the spirits had drunk the wine, presumably. The employee quickly ran out of the building and resigned immediately. Another strange occurrence in the restaurant is that candles will not stay lit. Once the candles are lit, they are blown out instantly with no apparent reason. One employee heard a woman's laughter coming from the Carlotta Salon while another claims to have seen a young woman wearing a black skirt and while blouse float into the Salon.

When the restaurant was being remodeled, all the rooms went smoothly except for the Carlotta Salon. Each morning all the new furnishings would be torn down and pictures strewn about the room. The owners were unsure if that room could ever be remodeled, but eventually the spirits gave in and seemed to like the way the room turned out.

Photos which are taken in Armando's old bedroom rarely come out, or the cameras fail to take a photo at all. Electrical malfunctions are common in that room as well; lights are turned on or off when no one is there to flip the switch.

Even though some speculate the validity of the lover's story, no one can challenge that ghosts reside in the restaurant.

Double Eagle Restaurant
2355 Calle De Guadalupe
Las Cruces, NM 88001
(575) 523-6700
www.double-eagle-mesilla.com

Raton

The Howarth Ranch

Just outside the mining and ranching town of Raton is a small house built in 1903. David Howarth, who previously owned a saloon in Blossburg, New Mexico, built the house when his wife became pregnant. Howarth and his wife had a large family, six girls and one boy. He thought it inappropriate to raise the girls in a saloon and sold it to take up ranching.

The girls grew up to be typical women of the era; many of the girls became schoolteachers in neighboring towns. After marrying, one started the local egg and chicken ranch, and three others married and moved away. Beatrice stayed home to manage the cattle ranch, and another, Anna, after a long teaching career, returned to the home ranch to live out her days.

Beatrice was known to sit on the front porch in the afternoon with a shotgun waiting for the many rattlers to slither near the house and to keep careful watch on the cattle.

Fred, the only boy, was born in 1889. He lived at the ranch helping with the cattle in his spare time, but worked in town as an Agricultural Agent. Fred enjoyed geology of the local area, and on one lucky occasion, found a mammoth tusk near Folsom. Fred died an unexpected and painful death when he was thirty-six from a ruptured gall bladder.

The Howarth family no longer lives on the ranch but their spirits still do. The transparent image of an older woman has been seen sitting on the porch in a phantom rocking chair, shotgun resting across her lap. An occasional shotgun blast has been heard through the valley coming from the vicinity of the house. A shadowy figure has been seen in the back room of the bunkhouse pouring over books and artifacts, and an occasional local rancher has seen this same figure walking along, picking up rocks, or digging in the ground as if looking for something. Is Fred still on his quest for interesting geological items?

The house itself has had strange happenings. When the last of the daughters died in the 1990s, the house was still primitive. Only a toilet had been installed in a storage room, but no sinks or faucets were added. Some say that Beatrice did not want any changes made to the house her father had built. Whenever modernization was discussed, a cold feeling would come over the room and an air of disapproval would be felt.

The caretaker, upon opening the house, has on several occasions smelled freshly baked bread, especially after the house has been closed for several days. Laughter is heard coming from the dining room as well as clinking of glasses and flatware against plates as if a phantom supper was happening. Doors are seen opening and closing, and the old hand water pump in the kitchen has been heard pumping with no movement coming from the pump itself. An occasional glow of an oil lamp and of a fire burning in the fireplace has been seen through the windows. It seems the Howarth family is still at home in the small ranch house.

Candlelight has been seen at this Raton ranch house when no one is home.

Route 666

Is US Route 666 the devils highway or is it just an urban legend? The infamous road travels from Gallup, New Mexico, all the way up through Colorado and then finally ends in the state of Utah. We are going to concentrate on the part of Highway 666 in New Mexico. The highway is commonly called the "Devils Highway" because of the scripture which identifies the number with the beast according to the *Bible's* Revelation. "Here is wisdom. Let him that hath understand count the number of the beast: for it is the number of a man; and his number is six hundred and sixty-six" (Revelation 13:18).

Over the years, many strange occurrences have happened on this lonely road in the northern part of New Mexico. A phantom car appears during a full moon running a motorist off the road. At least five deaths are blamed on this evil vehicle and many accidents. A pack of wild dogs have been seen running down the highway; anyone who stops for these dogs has their tires shredded by their sharp teeth. The dogs are described as having yellow glowing eyes and are only seen at night. An apparition of a thin looking woman in a nightgown appears as well; she flags down motorists but always disappears. An unusual number of bodies have been found dumped near the roadside and the highway holds the highest number of auto-related accidents in the state.

Keep your eyes open when you are driving on Highway 666.
Courtesy of BigStockPhoto

One man recounts a frightening trip he took on the "Devils Highway." In the middle of the night, he was traveling by himself down this roadway heading for Gallup. At the horizon, he saw a semi-truck traveling down the middle of the road at such a high rate of speed that he pulled off the road immediately and ran about twenty feet into the desert to avoid this truck. He described it as being on fire, sparks dancing around its wheels and flames shooting out from its smokestack. He waited for the truck to pass, surely slamming into his car, but it continued on its journey from hell. The man returned to his car, took a deep breath of relief, and continued without further incident to Gallup.

Another man had an eerie encounter during a drive on the highway. On a long drive from Sheep Springs to Gallup, a man spotted a female hitchhiker along the side of the road. She was wearing a blue floral button up shirt and jeans, and carried with her a well-worn jean jacket and backpack. She quietly entered the car and gave short answers to every question; the man persisted on the whole trip trying to strike up a conversation. She was polite but revealed little about herself, only staring at the crucifix that hung from the rear view mirror. Soon her destination neared and he let her out of the car without a second thought. About fifty miles further along the road there she was standing with her thumb out looking for a ride, but how could that be! No cars had passed the man and he did not stop anywhere. That's when he realized he had picked up the hitchhiking apparition he had heard about for so many years, and she must not have liked the crucifix that hung from the mirror for she disappeared when his car approached to pick her up again.

The Native Americans talk of Skin Walkers which can shape shift into animals and appear in front of your car causing you to swerve and sometimes crash; this may explain many of the unwarranted accidents along the road. This is thought to be a warning from the Skin Walker before he appears in your car. Many travel in groups so the Skin Walker will have nowhere to sit. Sometimes this fails as well, and it is said not to travel tired or alone or the Skin Walker will play all kinds of tricks on you and could be looking to steal your soul.

The signs that mark the highway seem to be a hot commodity; New Mexico residents often complain about the road and have petitioned many times to have the name changed. In 2003, Governor Bill Richardson did just that. Even though the name is now Route 491, don't be fooled. It is still the "Devils Highway."

Santa Fe

La Posada Hotel

La Posada Hotel originally was a grand mansion built by Abraham Staab in 1882 for his wife, Julia. The Staab family was a large one with six children. The children all had rooms on the second floor of the mansion with a ballroom on the third floor for the lavish parties Julia threw. Julia enjoyed being the social center of Santa Fe and her home showed it, furnished with the finest European furniture and trinkets.

Unfortunately, Julia's happiness quickly ended when her seventh child died soon after birth. Abraham thought that giving her more children might bring her out of her depression. After many unsuccessful pregnancies, the couple stopped trying and Julia became even more despondent. After a while, Julia scarcely left her room, her hair turned from a beautiful jet black to white almost overnight and rumors persisted that she had gone insane. Julia finally died at the age of fifty-two in 1896.

The rest of Julia's children grew up and eventually moved out of the mansion. Abraham stayed at the mansion until his death in 1913.

In the 1930s, the mansion was purchased and turned into a hotel, thriving for years in the small community. Arts programs and theater troupes used the mansion and grounds for their events without any odd happenings. However, in the 1970s, reports that Julia may still be around started surfacing.

Guests and visitors reported seeing a translucent woman all over the mansion. She would appear quickly and disappear just as fast. A hotel employee saw her once repositioning an armchair. It appears that Julia does more than just move chairs; glasses fly off shelves or move by themselves, fireplaces turn on and off on their own accord and visitors to the mansion have even taken photos of Julia's ghost.

La Posada Hotel
330 East Palace Avenue
Santa Fe, NM 87501
(505) 986-0000
www.laposada.rockresorts.com

Loretto Academy

When the Loretto Academy for women needed a chapel for their school, they chose the beautiful Saint Chapelle of Paris to use as a model. Built in 1878, the Loretto Chapel was plagued with problems from the start, including the unfortunate death of the main architect. The walls are built from local sandstone with the ceiling consisting of volcanic rock. The two large stained glass windows were created in Paris; on their way to Santa Fe the windows traveled to New Orleans, up to St. Louis, and then on the Santa Fe trail to their home in the chapel. When the chapel was nearly finished the carpenters noticed the late architect did not include a way to the choir loft. All of the stair ideas were refused by the sisters, stating they were either unsightly or would take up too much room. The builders deemed it impossible and the chapel was finished without a staircase.

The sisters started praying a Novena to St. Joseph, the patron saint of carpenters, for a solution. On the ninth and last day of the Novena, a strange carpenter appeared on a donkey carrying a toolbox looking for work. He promised the sisters that he could resolve their dilemma with just a small request, several tubs of water.

Each day the sisters would enter the church for prayers, the carpenter always withdrew during this time. Each day the stairs grew finally ending with thirty-three steps, the age of Christ when he was crucified. No nails or screws were used and no support was needed. The staircase, a double helix, added to the beauty of the chapel.

After completing the staircase, the mysterious carpenter could not be found for payment. The sisters put notices in the local paper asking if anyone had seen him. The local residents had not seen him before or after he had come to build the staircase. The sisters asked at the lumberyard; they had not seen him or sold him the wood. Upon inspection, the wood was not of the region and no one knew what kind of wood it was. The sisters of Loretto believed it was St. Joseph, himself, that came to build the staircase.

Who was the mysterious carpenter who built the staircase in the Loretto Chapel? *Courtesy of R.W. O'Brien*

The sisters were very grateful to have such a wonderful staircase to the choir loft but it was quite a scary task to climb and descend the steps. Built without railings the sisters would sometimes crawl up and down the stairs in fear of falling, later a railing was added for the safety of the sisters.

To this day, no one knows for sure who built the staircase, what wood it was made out of, and how it is able to have two 360-degree turns without support. Only wooden pegs hold the stairs together.

Loretto Chapel
207 Old Santa Fe Trail
Santa Fe, NM 87501
(505) 982-0092
www.lorettochapel.com

Santa Fe Pueblo

It is unknown when the adobe pueblo was built, speculation leads us to the thirteenth century, but today it is known as the oldest house in America. The Indian community existed from around 1200 AD to 1435 AD, but the entire area was abandoned when the community moved farther south. The pueblo sat empty for more than 160 years, when a group led by Don Juan de Onate brought 950 settlers to the area in 1598. The town was split into two groups, the European and the Tlaxcalan Indians in what is now Santa Fe.

Over the years the pueblo housed Franciscan missionaries, served as an infirmary during the Pueblo Rebellion of 1680, and then was occupied by the victorious Pueblo Warriors. After the warriors moved on, the pueblo housed the Spanish governor, was used as different shops and residences for every class of people, and once was the residence of witches.

During the late 1600s, Juan Espinoza, a Spanish soldier, found himself in Santa Fe. Like many small towns at that time, a young woman would have seen such a man as the catch of the century. Soon after arriving, Juan fell in love with a beautiful young woman. He had planned on marrying her. When Juan proposed, she refused and claimed she was to marry another much wealthier man.

Juan was heartbroken and sought the help of two witches who resided in the Santa Fe pueblo. Blinded by love, he asked for a love potion to bring the girl back into his arms. The two witches brewed up a concoction and promised it would bring the girl back to him. This task was not cheap and the witches demanded a hefty payment.

Despite the love potion, the woman married another man. Juan was furious and returned to the witches to insist a refund. The witches refused, Juan pulled his sword and lunged at the witches, and as they ducked out of danger one threw out her leg and tripped Juan. His sword slipped out of his grasp and without hesitation, one of the witches snatched the sword up and severed his head completely off.

Juan Espinoza is still seeking revenge for his losses. Especially in the month of April, his headless ghost is seen searching for his head. Juan is most commonly seen riding an unearthly horse down the street that runs into the Santa Fe River, brandishing his sword over his head.

La Llorena

All throughout the Southwest and Mexico, children have been hearing the legend of La Llorena. There are several different versions of this tale depending on where you live and who tells it. My favorite version is about Maria, a beautiful but very poor woman in the early 1700s. She had many suitors and Maria's mother urged her to make a good life with one of them, but she refused, waiting for a rich man to notice her charms and sweep her off her feet.

It was not long before such a man came along; he was the son of a wealthy rancher, and very handsome as well as charming. The courting did not last long before they were married. The happy couple moved to a ranch outside of Santa Fe and settled into a familiar life. Besides working on the ranch, he also worked as a merchant, leaving the beautiful Maria alone to tend to their three children.

As the years passed the once happy couple started to grow apart. With her husband leaving for longer and longer periods, Maria started to wonder if he was enjoying the company of other women. One day, Maria and her children were walking in town when her husband's buggy appeared. Her excitement ended when she saw his companion, a beautiful woman whom he was sitting shockingly close to. The buggy passed and it was obvious to Maria he was pretending not to notice his wife and children. Maria was heartbroken.

She spent great lengths of time replaying what must have gone wrong, how could she get him back? One day in a rage, she decided if she didn't have children, her husband would love her again. In haste, she dragged her three children to the roaring river and threw them in.

She returned home to her husband and told him what she had done, thinking he would be pleased, but instead he was horrified and sent her away, never to be with him again. Maria realized what she had done, and fled frantically looking for her children, calling out and crying for them through the streets and down by the river. Having found no sign of them after several days, and having lost everything, she went down to the river and drove a dagger into her own heart.

Soon after her death, her spirit continued to roam the banks of the river looking for her children. At night, her wails echo throughout the region, terrifying the local people. Soon no one wanted to venture out in fear she would come after them. Night after night, her wails were heard. Soon people started calling her La Llorena, The Weeping Woman.

For centuries Maria has been seen roaming the nearby rivers crying for her children. If you see her, she may ask you, "Donde estan mis hijos?" (Where are my children?). She has been known to pull children into the river if she finds them, mistaking them for her own. She appears beautiful from afar, but if you dare to get close enough, she turns into a rotting shell of a woman.

Many people think the story is brewed up by parents to keep their children away from the water. Although this may be so for some people, La Llorena does exist. In the 1930s, a small boy was playing along the Rio Grande when he encountered her. It was late in the afternoon when the sun quickly set and he was all alone with just the illuminating moonlight. All of a sudden, the boy saw a ghostly white form rise from the river, near where he was playing. Then a scream echoed all around him. "Mis Ninos!" Struck with fear he could not move. He just stood there in silence as the ghostly woman, with empty eyes in a long rotting face, and tangled black hair reached out her bony hand and again cried, "Mis Ninos!" The bony fingers grabbed his wrist and slowly pulled him closer to the water. Closer and closer, he was pulled to the water, powerless with fear to fight back. Suddenly, church bells filled the night; the startled La Llonena loosened her grasp on the boy. He quickly realized what had happened and ran home. His mother was infuriated with the boy, until she saw how white with fear the boy was. He was not taken to a watery grave by La Llorena but had a bruise on his wrist from her bony fingers to remind him not to play by the water.

La Llorena still cries for her children down by the river, but over the years she has widened her search to rivers and streams all over the southwest. Keep your offspring close; you never know when she will come along looking for children.

Taos

The Alley Cantina

Dating from the 1600s, the Alley Cantina was originally built by Pueblo Indians as an outpost along the Chihuahua Trail. When the Spanish arrived, they used the adobe building as offices, and later Charles Bent, the first Territorial Governor, was beheaded by a mob in 1847. It is Bent's daughter, Teresina, that is said to haunt the restaurant.

Bent came to Taos in 1835, and settled down with Maria Ignacia Jaramillo. The couple had five children and was later related to Kit Carson, when Carson married Maria's younger sister, Josefa, in 1843.

Bent was a well-known merchant in Taos and had made many enemies because of his condescending view of the local Hispanics. On one occasion, Bent watched as a local man was whipped in his home and was later driven out with his family in the middle of the night by four masked men who entered through the front door. Bent was thought to have hired the four men to drive the Hispanic man out of town.

The Mexican-American war broke out in 1846; troops were sent to New Mexico and California to gain control and quickly did when Governor Manuel Armijo fled to Santa Fe. The new American governor was Charles Bent. Many New Mexicans were not pleased to lose connection with Mexico and were afraid of losing their land. In fact, many of them did.

It wasn't long before a rebellion was in the works and Governor Bent received word of a conspiracy. Seven men were arrested but it was not long before Bent was murdered in his home along with his brother-in-law. Sheriff Stephen Lee, Judge Cornelio Vigil, and several others were murdered in their homes that night as well. In the months following, the rebels were captured and after a quick trial executed. The rebellion finally ended six months later in July 1847.

Bent's daughter, Teresina, has been seen in the restaurant by staff and diners. Reports of a translucent young woman in white are abundant among visitors to the popular eatery. Teresina is to blame for the many accidents in the restaurant. Plates fall off customer's tables; drinks have been known to spill or disappear, and chairs move unexpectedly. In the kitchen, the sounds of pans toppling have been heard; when the staff go to investigate the noise, nothing has moved. Why does the former Territorial Governor's daughter stick around his old office long after she's passed? Perhaps one day she will give a clue; maybe she just likes the live music and friendly locals.

The Alley Cantina
121 Teresina Lane
Taos, NM 87571
(575) 758-2121
www.alleycantina.com

The Rio Grande Bridge

He parked in the middle of the bridge, placed his wallet, keys, and goodbye note on the driver's seat and walked to the railing. After looking down for a moment, he crawled over the railing and pushed off, falling 650 feet into the river and rocks below. His body was found a few days later a half mile downstream.

Northwest of Taos, New Mexico, is the Rio Grande River Gorge; spanning the gorge on Route 64 is the beautiful Rio Grande Bridge. It stands over 650 feet above the river and is one 1,280 feet long. Once known as the "Bridge to Nowhere," the bridge builders ran out of money in 1965, after building the cantilever truss to continue the road past the massive structure. The bridge now is a hotspot for ghosts who jumped to their death from the bridge.

Constructed as a walking bridge as well as a roadway, there is just a small railing keeping the despondent from jumping over. Today, there are talks of putting up netting or a higher railing to help deter the suicidal from jumping. Over the years, countless men and women have jumped over the railing thus ending their lives. In 2005 alone, seven people jumped to their deaths.

Have you seen the spirit of the girl on the Rio Grande Bridge?
Courtesy of BigStockPhoto

Many of these hopeless individuals still roam the bridge, their spirits encouraging others to jump and join their family of spirits. One of these spirits is seen quite often. A young Hispanic woman is seen walking on the bridge.

A New Mexico state trooper has seen her on more than one occasion. He was traveling west on the bridge when he passed a young woman walking. Thinking she may have had car trouble, he turned around as soon as he reached the other side. Cruising along slowly in his car he could not find the young woman—she had vanished. She couldn't have gone far. He stopped his car and shined his high powered light down at the river, everything seemed calm, no sign of her. Turning around again, he thought maybe he could find her car, upon traveling many miles down the road he never came across a vehicle. Thinking she may have jumped and washed down the river he set up a search party for her body. After a few days of not finding anyone, the search was called off.

The story might have ended with just a strange unexplainable encounter, leaving the trooper scratching his head but just a few months later he saw her again, and again she disappeared without a trace.

News of his encounter circulated among other troopers, and many of them came forward with their own stories of the young Hispanic woman walking on the bridge.

Hotel Martin/Taos Inn

Dr. Thomas Paul Martin and his wife, Helen, came to Taos in the 1890s and soon bought the largest house in a small plaza. He was well loved and was one of the few Taosenos that stayed out of trouble and was never involved in a scandal. After Doc's death, his wife bought up the neighboring buildings and opened the Hotel Martin in 1936. Today the inn is still open to guests and offers a restaurant and the famous Adobe Bar. The adobe building dates back to the 1660s and the fountain in the lobby used to be one of the wells for the town.

Arthur Manby owned the property at one time and sold Doc Martin his home. Manby was one of the greediest men to live in Taos, owning much of the land and property in Taos, but acquired most of it by less than honorable means. He was married several times, had lawsuits over land, and gold mine issues and was not well liked by most, but that's another story. In 1926, Manby was found beheaded in his house. No one came forward with any information on the murder, and today it remains unsolved. Manby's house is located next door to the hotel and still shares a common wall with the property.

The kitchen of the Taos Inn, as it is known today, seems to be where Manby's spirit stays on. An unseen hand has thrown appliances and a pan or two. Lights in the Inn turn on and off, doors open, and close forcefully, and occasionally strong cold winds blow through the kitchen area, startling the staff. Some of the guests and staff have even seen Manby wearing a faded leather jacket and a brown hat.

Although Manby causes the most activity in the Inn, other ghosts are present as well. It seems Helen might have stayed on. The smell of roses are often present, even in the middle of winter, and a tall thin woman has been seen in room 106 walking straight through the mirror, disturbing whatever dust may have settled on it. One room had figures painted on its fireplace; guests would refuse to stay in that room, feeling uneasy upon entering it. Painting over the figures seems to have done the trick, guests have not complained since.

The Adobe Bar has its own paranormal activity. After closing, employees hear their names called out and several apparitions have been seen, glasses move and chairs rearrange themselves when your back is turned. After a few drinks, you may think you've just forgotten where you've put your drink, but it was probably the spirits at the Taos Inn and Adobe Bar stealing a sip.

Taos Inn
125 Paseo del Pueblo Norte
Taos, NM 87571
(575) 758-2233
www.taosinn.com

Utah

Canyonlands

Dead Horse State Park

Dead Horse State Park is one of the most beautiful parks in Utah, surrounded by steep cliffs with the Colorado River running below. It is breathtaking. Many hikers come each year to the park to take in its beauty and exciting trails. One couple got more than they were asking for on such a hiking trip.

The couple wandered off the trail and quickly got lost as so many do in the park. Soon it grew dark and they decided to stop for the night and make camp, not wanting to try and find their way back in the dark and risk falling off a cliff. As the couple rounded a bend looking for some sort of shelter, they stopped dead in their tracks as they came across a group of Indians camped in a small alcove in the cliff side. An older man was sitting by the fire eating while a woman, presumably his wife, tided up and set up sleeping places. A young boy about five or six years of age played nearby. The Indian family did not look up; they continued about their business and did not notice the lost hikers. The whole Indian scene faded away slowly before their eyes.

Right:
Did lost hikers come across a residual haunting in the canyons of Dead Horse State Park?

Courtesy of R.W. O'Brien

Courtesy of R.W. O'Brien

Courtesy of R.W. O'Brien

Courtesy of R.W. O'Brien

The couple was confused, they stepped into the alcove and looked for signs of the Indians, nothing was to be found. Deciding this was the perfect shelter for them to spend the night they soon made camp and fell asleep.

The next morning the hikers looked closer at the camp and noticed on the wall old soot marks from where a fire once burned. A small turquoise bead and an arrowhead was also found.

They continued on their way and eventually spotted a few rangers who had come out to look for them. They spoke to one about what they encountered and he said others reported similar experiences as well.

Lake Powell

Lake Powell is the second largest man-made lake in the United States. Before the dam was built, Lake Powell was home to Native Americans who felt the river was a sacred spot. The ancient riverbed is riddled with petroglyphs. Many Indians were buried along the banks which the lake has encompassed. Only the Navajos and Paiutes once used the land these sites sit on. Thousands of visitors now use them each year and they are now known as Bullfrog, Page, Wahweap and Hall's Crossing.

The Navajo Indians alone lost at least two sacred places. When the dam was built, it backed up the flow from two rivers, the Colorado River and the San Juan River. The confluence of the two rivers was a sacred place to the Navajo Indians. These rivers met to create water children of the cloud and rain people. Just around the corner from where the rivers join is a natural rock arch, Rainbow Rock Arch National Monument, which is said to be the male and female holy beings that created clouds, rainbows, and moisture. This site is no longer used in religious ceremonies; instead, tourists leap from the edge of the rainbow bridge into the waters below, and the water of the lake itself is eroding the foot of the bridge.

Another site that is lost below the waters of Lake Powell is the Hole in the Rock Trail. The trail was created by the Mormons in the 1880s. Rock art panels that were created by the Anasazi Indians are also underwater now.

Spirits of Indians still dance among the rocks at Lake Powell. *Courtesy of BigStockPhoto*

Recreationalists in the area hear flute playing in the distance and laughter. When the visitors to the area try and find the source, they are confused as the music always seems just a bit off in the distance. No source to the sound has ever been located. Occasionally, a boater in the area will see a lone American Indian walking along the red sandy shoreline, or up on the rocks that protrude out of the waters. The Indian always seems to be looking for something and then just fades away.

Minersville

Minersville Creek

A mysterious woman in black haunts the creek near the town of Minersville. She was once very wealthy, no doubt from the copper and lead mines nearby. She was quite flamboyant and many around town knew of her great wealth. Rumors started spreading that a group of hoodlums were planning on robbing her. Once the woman got wind of this, she hid her money somewhere near Minersville Creek. The robbers were determined and tried to extract the location of the money from her, torturing her; she refused and in their haste, they killed the poor woman. She wanders the area protecting her money from treasure hunters. The money has yet to be discovered, but if you go looking for it beware of the lady in black.

Nephi

Phantoms

Nephi was settled in 1851 by the Mormons, the town was plotted and called Salt Creek for the nearby salty stream. Schools were built and the town was on its way; soon it became the Juab County seat. In 1889, Salt Creek was officially changed to Nephi, which came from the book of Mormon. Agriculture and mining were the town's staples, the railroad soon came, and it seemed it was going to keep growing. However, with the modern-day highways heading to larger communities, the town slowly started to dwindle. The town is still there and in 1980 reached its highest population of 3,285. Nephi Canyon is located just outside town on Highway 132, on the way to Fountain Green.

A local man of Nephi had a hair raising experience while driving his truck on Highway 132 through Nephi Canyon. One morning he headed out to Fountain Green driving his sturdy 1970s Chevy truck. He noticed out his window a group of three Indians dressed as warriors on horseback. They were armed with bows and arrows just a few hundred yards from the road traveling towards the mountains. He thought they were looking for something, perhaps they were on a hunting trip. The Indians even looked in his direction but did not seem to notice him. He continued to watch them until they just seemed to slowly fade away.

He thought it was unusual but didn't think much more about it until a large black shadow in the shape of an old wagon pulled by oxen came out of nowhere a few more miles down the road. The shadow started getting closer until it seemed to be on top of the truck, the truck slid across the road as if a strong wind had pushed it but it was not a windy day. The truck almost veered completely off the road and the man slammed on his brakes. The shadow kept on going. The truck had no problem when he returned to the road. Was that a phantom wagon that pushed the man around on the road?

Mountain Meadow Massacre

Not far from Nephi is where the famous Mountain Meadow Massacre took place. In 1857, more than 120 unarmed men, women, and children were slaughtered. No one will ever know for sure what really happened to the wagon train full of emigrants traveling to California from Arkansas.

Tensions were high between the Mormons and the United States government at that time. A few of the Mormons thought the government sent the group, or had ulterior motives, a one sided "war" broke out in the meadows. Painted like Paiute Indians, a small group of Mormons and real Paiute Indians opened fire. The wagon train was moved into a circle so that the group could defend themselves but they were unsuccessful. With food, water, and ammo deplenished the group was getting desperate. Several men were killed during the initial attack; the ones who remained were persuaded to give up their weapons and told they would have safe passage to Cedar City if they left their wagons, guns, and belongings. With no other choice and under heavy guard, they made their way about a mile up the canyon, when suddenly their benefactors, the Mormon men, opened fire on them.

Spirits still travel through the once beautiful Mountains Meadows.
Courtesy of Library of Congress, LC-DIG-pga-00322

In just a few minutes the peaceful group was dead, including thirty-five children. Only seventeen of the children survived that day and were placed with Mormon families, and later returned to relatives in Arkansas. The wagons and all of the victim's belongings were auctioned off at the Latter Day Saint Cedar City tithing office.

The men that died during the initial attack were buried in the circle of wagons, the other members of the party lay for two years decomposing in the open field and were later buried by the United States Army in several large graves. A memorial now stands in the Meadows.

No one can be sure what really happened that fateful summer in Utah. The meadow has never been the same, once a beautiful rich area, the soil now is barren and sandy. The meadows that once existed when the wagon trains passed through are long gone. The local Indians believe the meadows are cursed and the wasteland which is left in the wake of the massacre is a reminder of the white man's evil ways.

Visitors to the meadows often report hearing agonizing moans and screams from seemingly nowhere. Unearthly voices are heard all over the area, screams echo through the valley when no one is around. Many visitors report an overwhelming feeling of sadness when they are in the meadows. Are these the spirits of the slain replaying the horrible five days over and over?

Silver Reef

Silver Reef sprang up nearly overnight as many mining towns do. In 1877, the boomtown had more than 1,000 miners looking for their fortunes. The main street was more than a mile long including six saloons, a hospital, boarding houses, grocery stores and a Wells Fargo office. Silver Reef was never a Mormon town although it was surrounded by Mormon settlements. The town only had a Catholic Church, which the Presbyterians were allowed to use for their services. Two years later the town had doubled in size and the local mines brought to the surface more than a million dollars a year. In 1881, the silver market dropped out and the mines were starting to flood. The miners were forced to move on to the next boomtown, and by 1890, Silver Reef was much abandoned.

Wells Fargo

The Wells Fargo office still stands along with a handful of other buildings which survived a fire in 1908. For many years the office served as a residence. Now the office is open as a museum and art gallery. Employees claim a dusty prospector haunts the old building. He is seen mainly lurking in the shadows. When the figure is approached, he simply disappears. Is this man waiting in the old Wells Fargo office for a package or is he just making sure the town is preserved?

Silver Reef Cemetery

Another area of Silver Reef where ghosts may lurk is the Silver Reef Cemetery. Visitors have seen a little girl in the cemetery; she is said to follow the strangers around looking for company or she may be curious about what the strangers are doing there. On occasion, if she takes a liking to you, she will follow you out of the cemetery to your car, but there are no reports she has ever gone home with anyone.

Some visitors to the cemetery have not seen the little girl, but instead hear footsteps and children asking to be taken home.

Are these children lost; do they know they are long dead? If you visit the cemetery be sure to check your back seat as you drive away; you wouldn't accidentally want to take home one of these long-lost phantom children.

Conclusion

The American Southwest was a hard cruel place, especially to the earliest settlers looking to find riches in the wild west. Many men found wealth and many more found death. After chasing dreams, some families found themselves torn apart, miners died from accidents or in gambling halls. Their wives were left with no way to support themselves; some turned to prostitution, many turned to drinking, drugs, and finally suicide. The children were left to run free; some grew up to become gamblers and gunslingers, other children died young of disease or accidents from living in lawless towns. The hard times these men and women faced left an everlasting imprint on the land they worked and lived on.

On vacations to the Southwest I remember looking at sand dollars left behind in Death Valley and I often wondered what other mysteries the land held. I later unearthed many phenomena that cannot be so easily explained as sea creatures in the desert, but so mysterious that they have been studied without conclusion. The desert may never reveal its secrets, but give only a glimpse of the answers it hides. Did the Mountain Meadow Massacre scar the earth forever? Are the kivas in Mesa Verde a portal to another spiritual plane? How are those rocks moving in Death Valley? I hope that these stories from the Southwest have piqued your curiosity and have given you an insight to the hard lives that helped form the hauntings that are left behind.

Next time you find yourself staying the night at an old hotel in the wild west, don't bother answering the telephone, it's only the resident ghost calling; be sure to sleep lightly; a lonely prostitute might nuzzle up to you in bed. For, you see, mysteries abound in the Southwest.

Bang, bang; you're dead...

Bibliography

Books

Bailey, Lynn R. *Tombstone, Arizona "Too Tough To Die" The Rise, Fall, and Resurrection of a Silver Camp; 1878 to 1990*. Westernlore Press, 2004

Branning, Debe. *Sleeping with Ghosts*. Golden West Publishers, Inc., 2007

Convis, Charles L. *Outlaw Tales of Nevada*. Morris Book Publishing, LLC., 2006

Dangberg, G. *Carson Valley: Historical Sketches of Nevada's First Settlement*. Carson Valley Historical Society, 1972

Dequille, Dam. *The Big Bonanza: An Authentic Account of the Discovery, History, and Working of the Comstock Lode*. Nevada Pubns., 1983

Enss, Chris. *The Lady Was a Gambler.* The Globe Pequot Press,2008

Garcez, Antonio R. *New Mexico Ghost Stories*. Red Rabbit Press, 2005

George, Wharton James. *Grand Canyon of Arizona, The: How to See It*. IndyPublish, 2005

Hudnall, Ken. *Spirits of the Border IV: History and Mystery of New Mexico.* Omega Press, 2005

Lankford, Andrea. *Biking the Grand Canyon Area*. Westcliffe Publishers, 2003

Loose, Warren. *Bodie Bonanza: The True Story of a Flamboyant Past.* Exposition Press Inc., 1971

Luhan, Mabel Dodge. *Edge of Taos Desert: An Escape to Reality.* University of New Mexico Press, 1987

MacKell, Jan. Noel, Thomas J. *Brothels, Bordellos, and Bad Girls: Prostitution in Colorado, 1860-1930.* University of New Mexico Press, 2004

Moran, Mark. Austin, Joanne. Sceurman. *Weird Hauntings: True Tales of Ghostly Places.* Sterling, 2006

Oberding, Janice. *Haunted Nevada.* Universal Publishers, 2001

Pacheco, Allen. *Ghosts Murder Mayhem, A Chronicle of Santa Fe: Lies, Legends, Facts, Tall Tales and Useless Information.* Lightning Source, Inc., 2004

Robson, Ellen. *Haunted Arizona, Ghosts of the Grand Canyon State.* Golden West Publishers, 2007

Schlosser, S.E. *Spooky Southwest: Tales of Hauntings, Strange Happenings, and other Local Lore.* Globe Pequot, 2004

Williams III, George. *Mark Twain: His life in Virginia City, Nevada.* Tree By the River Publishing Trust,1985

Young, Herbert V. *Ghosts of Cleopatra Hill Men and Legends of Old Jerome.* The Jerome Historical Society, 2001

Newspaper and Magazines

"Awful Catastrophe." *New York Times.* April 9, 1869

"Perils of Nevada Mining." *New York Times.* July 10, 1870

"Spirits of the Old West hang around ghost towns." *Los Angeles Times.* November 18, 2007

"The Legend of La Llorena, The Ghost of the Rio Grande." *El Defensor Chieftain.* December 1, 2007

"The Pacific Coast; Another Fire in the Nevada Mines." *New York Times.* April 14, 1869

"The Virginia City Fire." *New York Times.* November 5, 1875

"Spirits of the Old West hang around Ghost Towns." *The Seattle Times.* November 18, 2007

"Yesterday's Tragedy." *Tombstone Daily Epitaph.* October 27, 1881

Web Resources

http://aroundcarson.com/tags/ghostwalk
http://azstateparks.com/Parks/YUTE/
http://blog.wfmu.org/freeform/2008/01/death-valley-th.html
http://chass.colostate-pueblo.edu/magazine/2002/ghost-walk1.html
http://co.el-dorado.ca.us/stories/tommyknockers.htm
http://com.miami.edu/parks/tovar.htm
http://computer-vet.com/travel/vc/thenandnow/mackay.html
http://en.wikipedia.org/wiki/Calico,_California
http://ghosttraveller.com/utah.htm
http://goldfield.travelnevada.com/
http://grand-canyon-vacation-information.com/huala-pai-indian-legend.html
http://hauntsofamerica.blogspot.com/2007/11/haunting-of-mackay-mansion.html
http://hubpages.com/hub/The-Oldest-House-in-America
http://nevadaculture.org/nsla/index.php?option=com_content&task=view&id=759&Itemid=95
http://news.aol.com/article/ghost-hunters/475264
http://projectparanormal.org/articles/ghost-locations/9/tarabino-inn/
http://s8int.com/phile/giants21.html
http://sharlot.org/archives/history/dayspast/text/2004_08_29.shtml
http://socyberty.com/death/most-popular-suicide-sites-two/
http://theaccidentalghosthunter.blogspot.com/2009/03/swamper-ghost-tombstone-arizona.html
http://thingsyoushoulddo.com/arizona/hotel-monte-vista-winslow-arizona
http://tombstonebirdcage.com/birdcage.php3
http://wildwestgold.net/
http://www.666truth.org/
http://www.allthingsadventure.com/the-lost-dutchman-death-roll/
http://www.americanfolklore.net/folktales/ca4.html
http://www.arizonahighways.com/static/index.cfm?contentID=1140
http://www.arizonahighways.com/static/index.cfm?contentID=664

http://www.arizonahighways.com/static/index.cfm?contentID=885
http://www.arizona-leisure.com/superstition-mountain.html
http://www.arizonaparanormalinvestigations.com/journey.htm
http://www.bignosekates.info/bnkbordellos.htm
http://www.blackjackssaloon.com/blackjack.htm
http://www.brentberryarts.com/artist_info/tarabino_house.htm
http://www.bukisa.com/articles/45982_route-666-the-devils-highway
http://www.carson-city.nv.us/Index.aspx?page=1219
http://www.chicagotribune.com/travel/chi-deathvalley_rc_pmnov18,0,7217317.story
http://www.chronicleoftheoldwest.com/last_week_07-april.shtml
http://www.colossalcave.com/welcome.html
http://www.csicop.org/si/2003-11/i-files.html
http://www.desertusa.com/mag07/may07/billykidcountry.html
http://www.dream-link.org/spookyplaces/news.htm
http://www.fabuloustravel.com/usa/article/393/21935
http://www.findagrave.com/cgi-bin/fg.cgi?page=gr&GSmid=46827298&GRid=19436730&
http://www.ghost2ghost.org/?p=1067
http://www.ghostinmysuitcase.com/places/birdcage/
http://www.ghostinmysuitcase.com/places/superstition/dutch/index.htm
http://www.ghoststudy.com/new2/vc.html
http://www.ghosttowns.com/states/az/tombstone.html
http://www.ghost-trackers.org/birdcage.htm
http://www.ghost-trackers.org/twainmuseum.htm
http://www.ghosttraveller.com/Nevada.htm
http://www.haunted-adventures.com/hauntedhistory.html
http://www.hauntedbay.com/features/Bodie.shtml
http://www.hauntedcolorado.net/Durango.html
http://www.hauntedhoneymoon.com/hauntedplaces/hotelvendome.html
http://www.haunted-places-to-go.com/yuma-prison.html
http://www.historicnevada.org/CVwalkDriveMapfor-web06_1.pdf
http://www.hotelmontevista.com/hauntedhotel.php

http://www.insync-ghosts.com/
http://www.invink.com/newmex.html
http://www.ktvn.com/Global/SearchResults.asp?vendor=wss&qu=%22Haunted+Nevada%22
http://www.ktvn.com/Global/story.asp?s=9263016
http://www.latimes.com/travel/la-trw-ghost28oct28.pg,0,5686725.photogallery?index=3
http://www.law.umkc.edu/faculty/projects/FTrials/earp/earphome.html
http://www.leadville.com/history/holliday.htm
http://www.legendsofamerica.com/HC-WeepingWoman1.html
http://www.lorettochapel.com/
http://www.nevadamagazine.com/index.php/issues/read/vintage_decor/
http://www.newmexico.org/western/experience/maria_teresa.php
http://www.newmexico.org/western/explore/elizabethtown.php
http://www.newmexicobeautiful.com/north-central-tourism/rio-grande-gorge.html
http://www.nmmagazine.com/links_directory/index.php?id=292
http://www.nvgenweb.org/storey/forts.html
http://www.offbeattravel.com/taos-new-mexico.html
http://www.ohjohnny.net/quotesabout/quotesabout.html
http://www.ohwy.com/nm/s/stjameho.htm
http://www.oldwesthistory.net/page36.html/
http://www.onlinenevada.org/julia_bulette
http://www.onlinenevada.org/yellow_jacket_disaster
http://www.parks.ca.gov/default.asp?page_id=21622
http://www.pvtnetworks.net/~gcs/lcf/hauntedplaces.html
http://www.religioustolerance.org/lds_mass.htm
http://www.ripleysghosttowns.com/goldfield.html
http://www.roadsideamerica.com/story/11288
http://www.ruidoso.net/
http://www.sangres.com/newmexico/colfax/elizabethtown.htm
http://www.snopes.com/horrors/ghosts/loretto.asp
http://www.spartacus.schoolnet.co.uk/WWearpV.htm
http://www.spirithunter.net/
http://www.spookyplaces.net/stories-2.html
http://www.strater.com/display.php?id=1

http://www.suite101.com/article.cfm/ghosts_and_haunted_spots/26520
http://www.superstitionmountainmuseum.org/lost-dutchman
http://www.taosinn.com./
http://www.territorial-enterprise.com/
http://www.theoutlaws.com/ghosts3.htm
http://www.toursofoldtown.com/ghosttour.php
http://www.travellady.com/Issues/September03/TrickorTreat.htm
http://www.trutv.com/library/crime/notorious_murders/classics/haunted_crimescenes/8.html
http://www.unexplained-mysteries.com/forum/index.php?showtopic=70064
http://www.usatoday.com/travel/destinations/10great/2006-07-27-10-great-haunted-hikes_x.htm
http://www.visitcampverde.com/camp_verdes_50th.php
http://www.visitcarsoncity.com/tours/carson_valley_drive.php
http://www.weirdnewmexico.com/stories/shorty02.html
http://www.xphomestation.com/nvsta-vansickles.html
http://www.yourghoststories.com/real-ghost-story.php?story=4905

Index

Adobe Bar, 136-137
Albuquerque, 102-105
Alcalde, 105
Amargosa, Hotel 63-64
Arizona, 6, 8, 13, 15, 21-22, 29, 30, 33, 44, 46, 106
Asylum Restaurant, 27
Big Nose Kate's Saloon, 38-39
Birdcage Theater, 35-36
Bisbee, 8, 10, 12, 14-15, 36
Bismarck Mine, 60
Bodie, 7, 48, 52, 54-55
Bodie Cemetery, 55-56
Boothill, 36-38
Böttger Mansion Bed and Breakfast, The, 103-104
Brewery Gulch, 8, 12
Cain House, 52-54
Calico, 57-61
California, 6-7, 42, 48, 57, 66, 77, 82, 90, 133, 146
Carbon Junction, 70
Carson City, 78, 82, 89, 93
Cimarron, 106, 108, 115
Cleopatra Hill, 21, 26
Cloudcroft, 109, 110
Colorado, 6, 42, 67, 75, 125
Colorado River, 19, 47, 138, 144
Colossal Cave, 14-15

Columbian Hotel, 68
Comstock, 82, 93, 95-97, 99
Connor Hotel, 24-25
Copper Queen Mine, 8
Crystal Palace, 40-41
Cuchillo, 110, 113
Cuchillo Bar and Hotel, 110-113
Dead Horse State Park, 138
Death Valley, 6, 61, 63-64, 150
Death Valley Junction, 63-64
Devils Highway, 125-127
Devils Racetrack, 61
Diamond Belle, 69
Double Eagle, 122-123
Douglas, 15
Durango, 67-71
El Tovar Hotel, 20-21
Elizabethtown, 106, 113-116
Ellis Store, 118, 120-121
Flagstaff, 17, 21
Flowery Hill, 95
Fountain Green, 145-146
Gadsden Hotel, 15-17
Genoa, 82
Genoa Bar, 82
Gold Hill, 85-87
Gold Hill Hotel, The, 85-87
Goldfield, 89
Goldfield Hotel, 89
Grand Canyon, 7, 11, 19-20
Grand Hotel, 38-39
Granite Gap, 116-118
Hank's Hotel, 60
Home Comfort Hotel, 75
Hopi House, 20
Hotel Martin, 136
Hotel Vendome, 29-30
Jerome, 21-28
Jerome Grand Hotel, 25-28
Lake Powell, 144-145
La Placita Restaurant, 102-103
La Posada Hotel, 127-128
Lambert Inn, 106, 115
Lane House, 60

Lil's Saloon, 60
Lincoln, 118-121
Lincoln County Courthouse, 7, 119-120
Lone Mountain Cemetery, 78, 82
Loretto Academy, 128-129
Loretto Chapel, 128-130
Lost Dutchman Mine, 32-33
Lynch House, 87-88
MacKay Mansion, 99-100
Maria Teresa's Restaurant, 104-105
Mark Twain Museum, 101
Mendocini House, 54
Mesa Verde, 72-73, 150
Mesilla, 122
Mile High Grill and Inn, 22-24
Millionaires Club, 97
Miners Lodge, 87
Minersville, 145
Monte Vista Hotel, 17
Mountain Meadow, 146-147, 150
Nephi, 145-146
Nephi Canyon, 145
Nevada, 6, 55, 78, 90, 93
New Mexico, 6, 7, 42, 97, 102, 104, 115, 118, 123, 125, 127, 133, 134, 136
Nogales, 29
OK Corral, 34-35, 37-38, 41-43
Olds Barn, 84
Oliver House, 13-14
Ophir Mine, 93, 95
Phelps Dodge Mining Company, 8
Phoenix, 30
Pipers Opera House, 101
Poston's Butte, 46
Prescott, 29-30
Racetrack Playa, 61
Raton, 123
Riesen House, 85
Rio Grande River Gorge Bridge, 134-135
Route 491, 127
Route 666, 125
Ruby Mountains, 90-92
Salt Creek, 145
San Pedro River, 12

Santa Fe, 97, 118, 127-128, 130-131, 133
Santa Fe River, 131
Silver Nugget, 36
Silver Queen Hotel, 96-97
Silver Terrace Cemetery, 97
Silver Reef, 148-149
Silverton, 6, 67-68
Skidoo, 65-66
St. Andrew's Episcopal Church, 29
St. Elmo, 75-76
St. Elmo Hotel, 75
St. James Hotel, 106-108, 115
Strater Hotel, 67-69
Superstition Mountains, 7, 30-31, 32-34
Taos, 133-134, 136-137
Tarabino House, 77
Territorial Enterprise, 93, 101
Tombstone, 15, 29, 34-43, 106, 116
Tombstone Cemetery, 37-38
Trinidad, 77
Tucson, 14-15, 43
Turkey Creek, 43
United Verde Copper Company, 25
Utah, 6, 125,138, 148
Van Sickle's Station, 82
Velasco Pueblo, 43
Virginia City, 78, 82, 85-87, 93-101
Vulture Mine, 44-45
Washoe Club, 97-99, 101
Yellow Jacket Mine, 85-87
Yuma, 45-47
Yuma Territorial Prison, 45-47